TABOO TOPICS

TABOO TOPICS

Edited by Norman L. Farberow
Foreword by Gordon W. Allport

ATHERTON PRESS
70 Fifth Avenue, New York 11, N.Y.
A Division of Prentice-Hall, Inc., 1963

Published simultaneously in Great Britain
by Prentice-Hall International, London

THE ATHERTON PRESS BEHAVIORAL SCIENCE SERIES

General Editor
WILLIAM E. HENRY
The University of Chicago

Foreword

Mrs. Grundy, the guardian of our decency, is a remarkably versatile lady. She protects not only the front porch of our moral edifice, but also the corridors of our science. Some topics—among them sex, suicide, and death—she declares out of bounds because they offend her social scruples. Others—among them graphology, hypnosis, religion, and parapsychology—she bans because they offend her scientific priggishness. The lady is so alert to both social and scientific impropriety that over the years she has contrived to bowdlerize or banish from the province of psychology many topics of deep human concern. The present volume impertinently takes issue with Mrs. Grundy. Its authors have spent many years countering her taboos, even if with only limited success.

Where would the science of psychology be without its anti-Grundys? In the middle of the nineteenth century, Elliotson and Esdaile, by defying the medical societies in Britain, encouraged the study of hypnosis. Freud thumbed his nose at Queen Victoria and all her virginal sacred cows. William James was a delightful maverick, a pioneer in the study of paranormal phenomena and religious experience. James regarded reductionist psychology as so much "humbug" and offered us a vision of a pluralistic universe of psychological truth. McDougall shocked the profession by embracing four heresies: Lamarckianism, animism, the concept of the group mind, and parapsychology. The present volume follows the tradition of dissent. We should thank the editor, Norman L. Farberow, for jogging our present complacency.

You may say that in these days it takes no great courage to slap down Mrs. Grundy's moral priggishness. Does not every college sophomore take a turn at it? True, our culture is no longer so strait-laced as it was half a century ago. But there is still much ambivalence on discussions of, and research in, such topics as sexual behavior, suicide, and death. Wardell B. Pomeroy, Evelyn Hooker, and Herman Feifel make this abundantly clear. At the same time, each author notes the widespread public relief that generally comes with the candid and objective examination of these topics. Dark, existential symbols lose much of their threat when thus exposed.

It is more difficult to break through the taboos imposed by our scientific Grundys. The price paid in professional dislodgment is heavy. Gardner Murphy makes the point in his chapter on parapsychology. Helmholtz, he relates, asserted that absolutely no evidence, not even his own experience, could convince him of telepathy, "since it is manifestly impossible." The same closed-mind denial prevails today. Murphy laments that, whereas other authors of the present volume "are concerned with things with which decent people do not deal, I am concerned with things that do not even exist."

If we were to arrange in order the strength of the scientific taboo on topics treated in this volume, the series would probably be: parapsychology (most intense), graphology (less in Europe than in the United States), religion, hypnosis, and politics. The other banned topics (sex, suicide, and death) deal initially with social, not scientific, taboos, but in these cases, too, the social bar creates a scientific one.

Scientific taboos reflect current codes of responsibility. Broadly speaking, it is currently positivism (in the guise of operationalism, stimulus-response, or information theory) that sets the scientific fashion. However valuable its contributions, positivism tends to hold investigators in an intellectual strait jacket. As William Douglas points out, the form and language of communication among psychologists often become more important to them than their message. There is little latitude for imagination; there are no rewards for the free spirit. Every psychologist is expected to know in advance just what the human mind can and cannot do. It reacts to stimuli. To look beyond this dogma is heresy.

Not every heresy is, of course, fruitful; not every iconoclast of today is a scientific hero of tomorrow. Some taboo-breakers will end up in blind alleys. Others, at least in the early stages of their work, will produce results that seem obvious or equivocal. Although the present volume contains some facts and findings of consequence, it is to be regarded primarily as a discerner of new horizons.

Most of the taboo fields do, in fact, suffer a common handicap. Their data are hard to come by. Feifel reports difficulty in gaining access to patients with terminal illnesses. Pomeroy explains how hard it is to find personnel qualified to conduct objective interviews on sexual history. Hooker's report underscores the same predicament. Suicides, as Edwin S. Shneidman points out, are elusive. In all these regions of experience, reticence is encountered. Even where there is less danger of dissimulation and concealment, there are handicaps of method. Because of its subjective nature, the religious sentiment is hard to approach on any but a superficial level. The analysis and validation of handwriting seem still to defy strict scientific controls. Parapsychology suffers both from a meagerness of method and from a shortage of critical and open-minded investigators.

Yet, most of the authors report a weakening of barriers in

recent years, as well as improvement in method. It is now possible to gain a wider hearing. Improvement, however, is not yet sufficient to attract younger investigators. They fear that an interest in taboo topics will blight their professional careers.

If scientists hesitate, laymen rush in. They find all these topics singularly attractive, sometimes because they seem bizarre, but chiefly because they are in fact central to everyman's emotional existence. In itself, this popular appeal is a good thing, testifying as it does to the richness of the lode. Unfortunately, however, the attractiveness brings a swarm of crackpots to bedevil the investigator with their ignorant queries and offers of help. They want to tell him of their own experiences and prowess and have not the slightest interest in controls or safeguards. I myself have worked in two of the areas treated here (graphology and religion), and I know the price that the lunatic fringe exacts. Hence I sympathize deeply with colleagues who work in still-more-sensitive areas of investigation.

Emotional involvement is not confined to bystanders. In his chapter on hypnotism, John G. Watkins points out that the investigator himself has a heavy investment. His convictions must be sufficiently deep to sustain him in the face of public and professional disapproval. Watkins observes, for example, that, in the field of hypnotism, investigators are, as a consequence of this investment, strongly partisan. The rivalry is sometimes fierce. There is a similar partisan intensity in religion, graphology, and parapsychology. Perhaps this is true of all taboo areas. Although vigor of commitment is understandable and controversies unavoidable, what impresses me is the calm, objective, informative tone of these essays. They surely show that the pioneer in science need not himself be fanatic.

Emotional complications and strain arise in still another direction—from the adjacent swamps of charlatanism. Daniel S. Anthony points out that the cheap doings of popular graphologists make universities wary of the whole subject of handwriting analysis, in spite of its justified claim to serious, sustained scientific attention. The antics of meretricious mediums virtually ruin the chances for an unbiased reception of research in parapsychology. William Douglas makes clear that the excessive piety of some writers on the psychology of religion calls into question the objectivity of all writers. And no doubt the legends of arcane powers of Mesmer and Svengali bring research in hypnosis into disrepute. The peril is particularly acute when frauds ride on the coattails of Kinsey and Pomeroy, selling pornography slightly disguised or making unwanted "telephone surveys" on their own neurotic initiative.

The authors themselves are sensitive to ethical issues. They know that, especially in taboo areas, the investigator must be alert to harm that may come to his subjects. He must also respect their privacy and anonymity and avoid misrepresentation. Ethical standards are exacting. To violate them brings discredit on the whole profession.

Perhaps the cruelest strain on the investigator is the questioning of his motives, not only by laymen but by professional colleagues as well. "And just why are *you* so much interested in the occult, in sexuality, in perversions, in suicide, in death, in hypnosis, in religion, or whatever?" That this sly innuendo is difficult to bear, most of the authors testify. It takes courage and a tough hide to persist. I wonder why it is that the issue of personal motivation is never raised in nontaboo areas. Who cares what underlies the interest of "respectable" psychologists in choosing to devote themselves to psychophysics or to the behavior of the rat?

Finally, a word in defense of taboos. In an important sense, they all point to aesthetic and moral principles which, if observed, would, to most people's minds, stabilize and smooth the course of our common life. As the writers themselves point out, by studying suicide, we are not advocating it; by studying sexual behavior, we are not condoning libertinism; by studying hypnosis, we are not favoring manipulation as a way of life. And, if we take unavoidable liberties with prevailing scientific canons, it is not because we reject the ideal standards of sound research. Taboos are worthy admonitions, but should not shackle free inquiry.

All contributors, to borrow Charles E. Osgood's apt phrase,

show a distinct ability "to run uphill." None more than Osgood himself. His essay on psychology in international affairs may at first seem slightly out of line with its companion pieces, but it is not. He shows that peace research, like all other taboo topics, is an emotionally laden area. Scientific Mrs. Grundys, favoring the cozy fashion of detachment, frown on do-gooders who dare to bring psychology into contact with the precarious situation of contemporary mankind. But the thoughtful reader will find Osgood's vigorous application of psychological sense to the turbulent issues of public policy wholly admirable. Unless many psychologists and many statesmen join forces with him and his associates, our precious science may soon be blasted into the wild blue yonder.

I find hope and challenge in this book. Its level of discourse is objective; its authors are pioneers. By breaking through Mrs. Grundy's prejudices, both social and scientific, they are helping to liberate regions in the heartland of human nature hitherto banned from view.

Gordon W. Allport

Cambridge, Mass.
May 1963

Contents

Contents

Contributors

Gordon W. Allport, Ph.D., professor of psychology, Department of Social Relations, Harvard University, Massachusetts.

Daniel S. Anthony, lecturer, New School for Social Research, New York; director, Newark Human Rights Commission, New Jersey.

William Douglas, Ph.D., associate professor of psychology of religion, Boston University, Massachusetts.

Norman L. Farberow, Ph.D., co-principal investigator, Central Research Unit, Veterans Administration Center, Los Angeles; co-project director, Suicide Prevention Center, Los Angeles; associate clinical professor of psychiatry (psychology), University of Southern California School of Medicine, Los Angeles.

Herman Feifel, Ph.D., chief psychologist, Veterans Administration Outpatient Clinic, Los Angeles; associate clinical professor of psychiatry (psychology), University of Southern California School of Medicine, Los Angeles.

Evelyn Hooker, Ph.D., research associate, Department of Psychology, University of California, Los Angeles.

Gardner Murphy, Ph.D., director of research, Menninger Foundation, Topeka, Kansas.

Charles E. Osgood, Ph.D., professor of psychology; director, Institute of Communications Research, University of Illinois, Urbana.

Wardell B. Pomeroy, Ph.D., director of field research, Institute for Sex Research, University of Indiana, Bloomington.

Edwin S. Shneidman, Ph.D., co-principal investigator, Central Research Unit, Veterans Administration Center, Los Angeles; co-project director, Suicide Prevention Center, Los Angeles; associate clinical professor of psychiatry (psychology), University of Southern California School of Medicine, Los Angeles.

John G. Watkins, Ph.D., chief, Psychology Service, Veterans Administration Hospital, Portland, Oregon; lecturer, University of Portland, Oregon.

TABOO TOPICS

Introduction

Norman L. Farberow

Man is constantly striving to understand himself and his fellow man. Known, but not always taken into account, are the powerful influences which are constantly at work in his society and culture. These forces, operating in ways of which he is not generally aware, are always present, shaping and fashioning his actions, reactions, thoughts, and feelings. More is meant here than the familiar unconscious, filled with conflicts and dark, repressed drives, or the everyday stream of events filled with habits, apperception, forgotten thoughts, and dreams. Rather, it is the culture itself which provides a many-faceted structure for its members, developing in a well-defined, codified way, the rules to which they will conform. These rules find expression not only in written laws and regulations but include, and most often stem from, the unwritten folkways, customs, and especially taboos. The permitted and the prohibited, the do's and don't's, are de-

veloped by society for its members out of self-preservative, tradi-
tion-enhancing motives. The most venerable and the most powerful of these are the don't's, which are rooted in the mythology of
the culture—and these don't's are generally the taboos.

Obviously, understanding taboos in their myriad ancient
and, at the same time, newly evolving forms is essential. One
would suppose that these significant factors in our everyday lives
had already been subjected to thorough investigation. One finds
instead that taboos are apparently sufficiently powerful to resist
not only change but also scientific investigation. Special problems
arise within each of the taboo areas of study, problems which do
not usually appear in investigations of other aspects of man's
functioning. Yet, it may well be that such problems are more
legitimately significant than the subject matter of the research
itself. This book reports some of the pioneer efforts by scientific
researchers to challenge the quandary of research in emotion-
laden areas and to venture into the unexplored regions of taboo
topics.

But, first, what are taboos? Taboos are primarily backward-
oriented, for, by being essentially forbidding and prohibiting,
they tend to preserve the past and to control the impingement of
the future on the present. Of course, not all taboos are old. New
ones constantly appear, taking various shapes and forms as the
substance of the culture evolves, but they all serve the same goal
—preservation of the *status quo.*

"Taboo," also known as "tapu," "katu," and "tambu," as a
notion and force in society, was first noted by Captain Cook in
describing the Polynesian customs in Tonga in 1771 (*Encyclopaedia Britannica,* 1947). He outlined the kinds and forms of
taboo as they appeared in that culture. *Webster's New International Dictionary* (2nd ed., unabridged) defines taboo as something which is "set apart or [made] sacred by religious custom, or
forbidden to certain persons or uses; such as may be violated
only at the cost of release of evil-working magical force." It is
something "forbidden by tradition or social usage or other authority; strongly disapproved as conflicting with conventions or
settled beliefs, often among a particular class. . . ." It is "a

sacred interdiction laid upon the use of certain things or words or the performance of certain actions; the action of imposing or state of being subject to such interdiction. . . . The taboo is commonly imposed by chiefs or priests. . . . The use of taboos is found among most races of primitive culture." Taboos are, however, not the exclusive property of primitive cultures. They exist and exert powerful influences in all phases of the most advanced and highly developed civilizations.

The *Encyclopaedia Britannica* (1947) defines taboos as something which has been "marked off," implying that certain things are unsafe for casual contact or not to be idly approached. Sumner (1940), in his extensive discussion of folkways, defines taboos as "Things which must not be done. . . . The primitive taboos correspond to the fact that life of man is environed by perils. . . . The taboos carry on the accumulated wisdom of generations which has almost always been purchased by pain, loss, disease, and death." He refers to "four great motives of human action" —hunger, sex passion, vanity, and fear. Other taboos contain interdiction of what will be injurious to the group. Frazer (1922) describes the taboos on persons, acts, words, and things and indicates the common element of danger. It makes no difference whether the danger is real or imaginary, the purpose of the taboo is to protect against and, at the same time, to preserve the imputed spiritual force.

Freud (1913) has written extensively about some of the feelings which occur with taboos. He believes that taboos are primeval prohibitions forcibly imposed from outside and directed against the most powerful longings to which human beings are subject. The desire to violate taboos persists in the unconscious. This last concept is similar to Kierkegaard's formulation that "anxiety is a desire for what one dreads" (1946).

"Taboo" has two meanings, diverging in contrary directions. The first is "sacred," or "consecrated"; the second, "uncanny," "dangerous," "forbidden," or "unclean." The term "holy dread" expresses the feeling accompanying taboos. Freud holds that the earliest human penal system may be traced back to taboo; that is, first the violated taboo took vengeance; then the gods and

3

wronged spirits avenged; and, finally, society took over punishment of the offender.

Taboos are directed mainly against liberty of enjoyment and freedom of movement and communication. In some cases, they have an intelligible meaning and are clearly aimed at abstinences and renunciations. But in other cases their subject matter is quite incomprehensible; they are concerned with trivial details that seem to be of a purely ceremonial nature. Freud quotes Wundt's statement that taboos follow the rule that anything that is uncanny or provokes dread becomes subject to taboo.

The positive aspects of taboo have also been recognized. Much of the social code which taboo enforces has an obvious ethical value, acquainting man with the structure of the culture in which he lives and reminding him of the obligations he has to the community of which he is a part. Taboos legalize and strengthen morality. Sumner (1940) mentions that some taboos aim to protect and secure, whereas others aim to repress or exterminate. Taboos act selectively, he states, affecting the course of civilization and containing judgments as to social welfare.

Obviously, the researchers reporting in this volume are not against all taboos. In most instances, as scientists, they take no position on the nature of the taboo itself; rather it is the difficulty in *investigating* the taboos which they concentrate on. But, as members of society and human beings, they do make judgments and personal investments. Thus, when taboos continue or develop without useful society-enriching functions or facilitate self-defeating or self-destructive activities, questions should be raised about them. For example, some taboos on killing oneself help prevent the needless loss of life and support one against the self-destructive tendencies of frustrated aggression and frustrated symbiotic dependency. But other taboos may flood the person with feelings of shame, embarrassment, and guilt and may prevent the person or his family from getting the professional help he needs at this critical period.

The topics of this volume range through many areas—some social, such as sex, death, and peace; others more academic, such as parapsychology, graphology, religion, and hypnosis. At first blush, a discussion of peace and public affairs hardly seems likely to find its way into a volume about taboo topics. However, they are certainly emotion-laden areas and, in these times, powerful and important factors in man's increasingly nervous functioning in his concomitantly (and paradoxically) shrinking world and expanding universe. Peace, especially, has begun to be looked on with suspicion—perhaps a real commentary on our times. Even more of a commentary is a recent report in a newspaper column about "peace . . . now a dirty word." The columnist told of a university professor who had stopped urging his students toward research in attitudes and feelings about peace because of the possibility that their actions would be misunderstood and their reputations sullied. As the reader will quickly note, this is the complete opposite of Osgood's behavior in the areas of public affairs and peace. Osgood's presentation does not exactly parallel the others in a specific detailing of the problems of research in a taboo area. But it is very germane in demonstrating, as do the others, the recognition of a need for, and the personal investment in, the furthering of scientific understanding in peace, as well as the conviction that the application of psychological research know-how often provides the best approach to tension-laden subjects.

One of the interesting additional aspects of taboos is the dangerous force of "mana," which seems to incorporate two powers—first, to remind man of his prohibited wishes and, second, to induce him to transgress prohibitions in obedience to his wishes. Perhaps it is this touch of mana which magically enough has permitted the investigators to challenge the taboos and stimulated the researches discussed in the following pages. More likely, however, is it to be the result of the situation described by E.G. Boring (1961): "Science feeds on its own decay and dissent is the agent that starts new growth."

The difficulties encountered by each investigator in his studies are outlined in detail in the following pages. Some brief general comments, however, can be made. (1) The subject matter of the taboos itself arouses complex pressures and produces problems of varying depth and intensity of feeling. Death and sex, for example, present widely differing problems in data collection, validity, and reliability; locating subjects and getting their co-operation; and the like than do hypnosis, graphology, or para-psychology. The various kinds of taboos also involve personal, moral, or ethical questions in varying degrees. Investigations of sexuality arouses social reactions, but may be more acceptable to many of the professional community than the investigation of graphology or parapsychology.

(2) As has been noted before, magic is invariably associated with taboos. This magic invests not only the form of the tabooed word, thing, person, or act, but tinges persons who become associ-ated with them, even as remotely as scientific investigators. Cul-ture "protects" its taboos, and its defensive activities are seen in many nearly magical countermaneuvers, such as denial, a magical insistence that the problem does not even exist. People "pass away"; they do not die. Extrasensory perception is just too far beyond credibility, so why bother investigating?

(3) More often, the researcher's problems stem not so much from the attitudes of the public as from those of his colleagues, the supposed allies in his own professional community. This is frequently a mixed attitude. There is, on the one hand, the gen-erally encouraging statement of interest and agreement on the importance and need for the study, and, on the other hand, there are the snide questions and implications of personal in-volvement. And this, of course, raises the important question of the researcher's own abilities to tolerate the questioning, doubt-ing comments, and raised collective professional eyebrows.

This book grew from a symposium which was presented at the American Psychological Association meetings in New York City in 1961. Five of the chapters of this volume were presented at this symposium in papers by Feifel, Hooker, Murphy, Pome-roy, and Shneidman and Farberow. The volume was expanded by contributions from Osgood, Douglas, Watkins, and Anthony. Gordon Allport was invited to write a foreword.

It is hoped that the book serves a fourfold purpose. The first is to indicate the feasibility of research in emotion-laden areas. The second is to illustrate methods and procedures already used in research in some of the areas. The third is to stimulate the interest of the large and growing number of professional research workers—especially the younger, possibly more enthusiastic, graduate student or newly professional person—in the possibility of further research. The fourth purpose is to point out the potentiality of challenging areas in man's functioning (which is the responsibility of social scientists interested in human behavior) that await scientific investigation by yet-to-be devised techniques.

In all of the topics discussed here, the work has just begun. Much remains to be done in these and other affect-filled areas, and the opportunities for new, vigorous, enthusiastic, and insightful research are plentiful.

▪ Selected Bibliography ▪

Boring, E.G. *Psychologist at large*. New York: Basic Books, 1961.

Frazer, J.G. *The golden bough*. New York: Macmillan Co., 1947.

Freud, S. *Totem and taboo* [1913]. In J. Strachey (Ed.), *The complete psychological works of Sigmund Freud*. London: Hogarth Press, 1955.

Kierkegaard, S.A. *The concept of dread*. Princeton: Princeton University Press, 1946.

Sumner, W.G. *Folkways*. Boston: Ginn and Co., 1940.

Death

Herman Feifel

Nothing in life is to be feared. It is to be understood.
— *Marie Curie*

La Rochefoucauld, the seventeenth-century French moralist, said that man could no more look steadily at death than at the sun. But the reader will recall the legend of Perseus. He was able, without being turned into stone, to behold the head of the Gorgon Medusa reflected in a mirror given him by the goddess Athena. Thus, he succeeded in slaying the monster.

I have no illusions about our slaying the monster. I feel, however, that, as a result of our miniature mirror, we may be able to look him in the eye somewhat more squarely. When I conceived the study, I knew that the area of death was not quite so popular as Edgar Guest used to be. I did not anticipate, however, that the shade of Semmelweis would start rustling again. In kaleidoscopic manner, I shall touch on what I was trying to do,

what occurred, and certain implications drawn from my experience.[1]

Earlier work of mine in the sectors of mental deterioration
(Feifel, 1951), old age (Feifel, 1961a), and time (Feifel, 1957) had
guided my attention to the possible importance of man's ability
to grasp the concept of a future and, with it, death. Orientation
to future events, I conjectured, might play a more commanding
role in our present behavior than we assume (Feifel, 1961b). I
reasoned, also, that investigating attitudes toward death in the
seriously ill, an "experiment-in-nature," could provide an additional entryway to how individuals cope with severe threat, thus
enriching our understanding of adaptive and maladaptive reactions to stress and of personality theory in general (Feifel, 1959).
Experience has shown that certain problems can sometimes be
revealingly approached in their exaggerated manifestations.
Through study of pathology, illness, and men under stress, we
have learned many of our initial truths about normal functioning (Allport, 1960a). Moreover, because of suggested relationships
between mental illness and one's philosophy of life and death
(Feifel, 1955), I felt that exploration of this field might serve
to broaden therapeutic horizons.[2]

The avenue for obtaining patients was naturally the physician. At the outset, I was met with: "Isn't it cruel, sadistic, and
traumatic to discuss death with seriously ill and terminally ill
people?"—a legitimate enough query. I agreed that a pilot study
was certainly in order. I was able to approximate my research
idea by being permitted to interview a number of mothers of
severely ill leukemic children. These interviews went well, but

---

[1] This paper is based in part on Research Grant M-2920 from the National
Institute of Mental Health, United States Public Health Service.

[2] Dr. Harold Searles, of Chestnut Lodge (Schizophrenia and the inevitability
of death. *Psychiat. Quart.,* 1961, 35, 631–665), has expressed a similar orientation. As a consequence of clinical work with schizophrenics, he postulates
that one of the major sources of anxiety against which the schizophrenic
unconsciously defends himself is the idea of mortality. Certain aspects of
schizophrenic symptomatology, e.g., the frequent feeling of not being alive
(hence not having to fear death) and the fantasy of personal omnipotence
with its implications of immortality, are certainly congruent with such a
conceptualization.

still no patients were forthcoming. Incidentally, this was in a hospital where a good proportion of the patients themselves recognized that the procedures being carried out on them represented somewhat final hopes concerning their condition.

After "gamesmanship" of an order that would have warmed Stephen Potter and with the valiant help of one of the staff physicians, I was enabled to interview and test eight seriously ill patients. The surmise would have been that the habitual drawbacks accompanying interview-data collection would be compounded here because of the nature of the subject matter. Contrariwise, not only were there no untoward incidents, but an unanticipated felicitous by-product was the seeming psychotherapeutic effect on some of the patients as a result of discussing their attitudes toward death. Still, no cooperation or even a laissez-faire attitude on the part of the hospital authorities was in evidence. I thought that perhaps an extension of the number and type of patients involved as well as the added participation of a consultant and staff psychiatrist might make for more impact. Again, with the support of an understanding oncologist, another ten patients were quarried out and interviewed. Once more, the refreshing frankness and cooperativeness of the patients involved were manifest. Some even thanked me for affording them the opportunity to examine their feelings about death. Characteristic responses were, "You helped me understand my feelings about death," "I'm grateful because I now have more control over my ideas," "You didn't avoid those things that concern me," "You cleared the cobwebs from my mind," "Talking to you gave me a sense of relief." These reactions were undoubtedly enhanced by the prevailing research context of viewing the patient as a human being with wishes, fears, and hopes, rather than as a diagnostic classification case of lung cancer or myocardial infarction.

Most seriously ill and terminally ill patients generally prefer honest, plain talk from physicians and family about the seriousness of their illnesses. They want to voice their doubts, affirm their faith, and communicate what their impending separation means. They do not want their problems ignored or reassurances they perceive as falsehoods. They feel supported rather than terror-stricken when they can express their sensibilities about death. In the writer's sampling thus far (N = 60), the great majority (82 per cent) desire to be informed about their condition in order to "Settle my affairs," "Make various financial and family arrangements," and because "It's my life—I have a right to know," "Would do what I really want," "Understand why I was suffering," "Would respond to treatment better if actually knew what I was up against," "Don't want to be denied the experience of realizing that I am dying," "Would have time to live with the idea and learn to die." Indeed, some recent studies suggest that terminally ill patients, when told of their prognosis, manifest an adjustment equal to or better than that observed in groups of matched patients similarly treated who have not been so informed. Further, realization of possible death seems to give permission, even freedom, to some to be themselves rather than extensions or mirrors of other people's values. Nevertheless, despite this reinforcing positive outcome, the light continued red.

Initially, this was perplexing, frustrating, and irritating to me, since the negative verdict was not allied to shortcomings in the experimental design of the problem, the unsuitability of the scientific procedures used, or the competence level of the researchers—all being certified diplomates in clinical psychology or psychiatry. The rebuff was based on the projected trauma to the patients and disturbance of their relatives that would occur, pilot studies notwithstanding. This repudiation was at first considered idiosyncratic, situational. After being vetoed a few more times—in varying setups, government and private hospitals, large and small institutions, by private practitioners and university medical schools—the realization began to sink in that what I was up against were not personal quirks, the usual administrative vicissitudes, nonacceptance of an inadequate research design, or pique at an outsider coming in to ruffle smooth waters. Rather, it was personal position, bolstered by cultural structuring, that death is a dark symbol not to be stirred, even touched—an obscenity to be avoided. I rememeber reflecting how paradoxical it was that the problem was turning out to be not the patient, but the physician, and that the researchers, propelled most likely by the same anxieties regarding death as the physician, should end up on an opposing side.

Some of the professional personnel contacted stated that they *never* told their patients they had a serious illness from which they could die. "The one thing you never do," they emphasized, "is to discuss death with a patient." Others said that people never think about death unless they are asked. Seriously ill individuals, a fortiori, are afraid to think about it, therefore, "we just don't ask them." There was this declaration from an associate professor of clinical medicine in psychiatry of a noted hospital: "No one is normal over age forty with regard to health, so I see no value to your study." This, by the way, was one of the very few reactions to the focus of the proposed research rather than to its content. From the acting research director of another hospital, there was this view: "How could you get a grant without your own subjects? You can't use our patients if you can't get them elsewhere." From the chief physician-in-charge of a leading metropolitan hospital, after three months of waiting, there came this answer: "Excuse my immoderate delay in answering, but you have to be a staff member"—a stricture just as well known to him at the inception of our discussion about obtaining patients. The commissioner of hospitals of one city responded with: "It is not consonant with our policy to set aside patients for this purpose." And then there was the chief research psychiatrist of a prominent medical center who "knew" that the research project would induce what he termed "test toxicity" in the patients, despite already demonstrated results to the contrary.

I must admit to more than passing vagaries about chucking the whole thing. Two things, though, held me to the task. One was my ego. I had made a dent or two, *mirabile dictu,* here and there, even convinced some that the idea was worthy of grant support—that is, after over two years of effort. Second was my sentiment, albeit occasionally dampened by the repeated rejections, that the study was significant and should, come hell or high water, be implemented.

Fortunately, there were also exceptions to the state of affairs I have been detailing. I did find congenial physicians and professional personnel who perceived what I was attempting to do, acknowledged its importance, and helped me get off the ground. There is no denying that the circumstances facing me did affect my original experimental design and forced me to compromise in ways I did not savor. I had envisioned, for example, certain kinds of independent behavioral rating criteria from observers in other disciplines, measures of the social matrix in which the patients found themselves, as well as data of a sequential nature. These aspects now had to be overlooked, if not forgotten. I found myself in the position of taking what I could get. Nevertheless, it is indeed an ill wind that blows no good. The negative responses to the research proposal themselves became grist for my research mill. Also, I noticed that I found energy and sustaining power from the fact of attack on a difficult situation— the key being confrontation, if not necessarily solution.

This leads me to another facet of work in the area—the researcher's own sensibilities about dying and death. One's own willingness to face or avoid the thought of death can be a relevant variable in the ensuing data. Few undertakings in psychological research, I think, are more emotionally exacting. Pain and death are themes not comfortably encompassed by categories of methodological rigor and theoretical relevance. Not only is the emotional resistance to the investigator, which I have been emphasizing, relevant to the research, but so also is the potential emotional scotoma of the researcher himself. The investigator is confronted with the Scylla of being affectively swamped—reactivation of his own anxieties about dying, antipathy toward or overidentification with certain kinds of patients, the sense of triumph at outliving some, guilt over inability to help others— and the Charybdis of overintellectualizing his approach, dissembling behind a façade of pseudorigorousness, and refusing to observe any but the grossest and least emotionally tinged dimensions of what is happening. Research on human behavior in extreme situations asks for a delicate balance of identification and intellectual detachment (Wallace, 1956).

Some implications of these strivings to advance comprehension of how consideration of death can serve life follow.

1. Death is a taboo subject in the United States, surrounded by disapproval and shame. The whole subject is unpalatable because it collides with strong notions concerning the uniqueness of life and finality of death. Freud (1925) has emphasized our resort to such "mischance" aspects of death as disease, infection, fortuity, and advanced age, thus betraying an eagerness to demote death from necessity to mere accident. Additionally, illness and death are considered not just bad fortune but imply overtones of personal failure and loss of status and identity. Fear of death is no longer so much the fear of judgment as it is fear of the infringement on the right to life, liberty, and the pursuit of happiness (Fulton, 1961). We cope with death by disguising it, pretending that it is not a basic condition of all life. We "exit," "cease," become "defunct," "demised," or "pass on"—but rarely die. Even when we do, our funerals are arranged more for the living than for the dead. Indeed, it is now a rare phenomenon for the average individual outside the medical and nursing professions to see an untreated dead person. A piece of domestic technology, for instance, familiar in most nineteenth-century households—how to deal with a corpse—has vanished. The whole business of death is gradually being bowdlerized out of common experience, giving place to the Gothic fantasies of horror films which now seem more acceptable to the public than details of the real thing (Lydgate, 1961). Prevalent entertainment treats death not so much as tragedy, but as dramatic illusion. One has only to recall the shock and incredulity of the Metropolitan Opera audience which saw Leonard Warren die on the stage.

Broadly speaking, Oriental man has a less frenetic approach to individual death because of philosophic and religious views which predicate a series of existences available to him in the future. Even those of us in Western culture who believe in some form of life after death hold that this earthly life is the *only* opportunity we receive to decide our fate in the "true" life to come. Be that as it may, maturity demands integration of the idea of personal death—recognition that dying and death are not separate states of being, but phases of the process of living and life.

Scientists and professional people are no less immune to prejudice than other groups—not only other disciplines but psychological colleagues as well. One recalls the important study of *The American Soldier,* where no attempt was made by the investigators to take advantage of the singular opportunity to examine the correlates of particular attitudes toward death. Although attitudes toward cowardice and fear were explored, the meaning of death as a possible component of these was overlooked (Faunce & Fulton, 1958). About two million persons die in this country every year. Nevertheless, not even a solitary paragraph on death is yet in evidence in any of our psychological texts. The partisan mind, it has been pointed out, has been standard human equipment for a long time. Opinionatedness, a priori personal judgment, undocumented assumptions, if not exactly idols of the den, still weave their entangling webs. Science does not march undeviatingly down an ever-broadening highway.

2. There are, clearly, impediments met by students of all behavioral phenomena whose character minimizes experimental manipulation. Nevertheless, as I have already implied, the very nature of some of the obstacles encountered in accomplishing one's research can be adapted to furnish fresh hypotheses and contribute new information. For instance, a hypothesis I developed as a result of my experiences was that one of the major reasons certain physicians enter medicine is to govern their own above-average fears concerning death. A study I have just completed on the attitudes of forty physicians toward death indicates that, though physicians think *less* about death than do two control groups of patients and one of nonprofessionals, they are *more afraid* of death than any of the control groups.

August Kasper (1959) has indicated that the physician considers his own fears about death, puts them as intellectual questions, and tries to answer them for other people. Phyllis Bottome's biography (1939) of Alfred Adler is also germane. She relates that he almost died from pneumonia at the age of five. The dread produced by this determined the boy to become a physician himself. In this way, he would be able to secure himself against the jeopardy of death. Dominion over his own anxiety would be obtained by having the power to cure. One must not minimize the demands made on the physician. Many are in constant contact with patients who arouse their own fears about dying and death, wound their narcissism, and impel them to palliate unabated calamity. Ministry to the dying is extremely difficult if we ourselves are not quite reconciled to the idea of personal death. It is also encouraging to note that the threat of death can function as an integrative, rather than disruptive, event for certain individuals. One can learn, apparently, not only to adjust to inordinate stress, but to grow and change under its spur.

We must be alert not only to the usual frames of reference —such as religious orientation, age, sex, time distance, and level of threat—but similarly to the special conditions of death. Knowing that you are suffering from a disease that will lead to death and remaining in your everyday environment with its regular duties and problems is quite unlike being immobilized, awaiting it in a hospital bed. For some, the manner of death rather than the mortal character of man is the key to the destiny of the individual spirit. Dying for an ideology or as the outcome of an auto accident may be distinct things. Norbeck (1961), for example, has indicated that, among the ancient Aztecs, the souls of warriors and male captives who were slain in sacrifice to their gods went to the most desirable of several available heavens. Those who died from sickness or in generally undistinguished fashion were assigned to a lower-grade one. Critical observation of the individual who is more ready than most people to die for principle can be insightful. Circumstances, social and cultural conditions, and personality factors are undoubtedly influential. If death represents loss of consciousness, self-control, and identity, then, psychologically, this type of individual avoids social isolation in eternity by identifying himself with specific cultural or religious values. He challenges death by emphasizing the omnipotence of a movement or cause. Likewise, there is the felt sense of triumph over death because he gives up his life when *he* chooses. The individual has, in a certain sense, made himself master over death. In another, he underlines the statement of Lao-tzu; "Who dies and, dying, does not protest his death, he has known a true old age."

One of the distinctive characteristics of our secular age, in contrast to the nineteenth century, has been transformation of the expectation of personal immortality into concern for historical immortality and for the welfare of posterity. Even this, Hans Morgenthau (1961) provocatively stresses, is now threatened by a potential nuclear holocaust. Such a war could destroy not only the individuality of death, but social immortality as well, by making both society and history impossible.

3. We err professionally in adopting a philosophy of *never* informing patients about the seriousness of their illness and undercutting talk about dying and death. An interesting contrast emerges in comparing studies of physicians and patients about whether to tell or not to tell. Sixty-nine to 90 per cent of physicians, depending on the specific study, favor not telling. In an opposing vein, 77 to 89 per cent of the patients want to know. Our outlook here may be too conditioned by the "healthy," rather than the seriously ill and dying themselves.

Not only patients, but most of us, feel less apart when we can share feelings and thoughts about dying and death. We recognize the mental-hygienic aspects of being honest in answering questions about birth. Research findings and clinical perception direct that we do the same for the topic of death. Naturally, how the telling is done is important. Truth can be cold and cruel, or it can be gentle, merciful, and hopeful. And telling must be suited to the needs and character of the individual. Some patients can suffer more from abrupt emotional isolation and unwitting rejection than from the illness itself. Many feel appreciative, not only because they can put their house in order, but because they have time to make confessions, either sacramentally or informally. Also, the opportunity to discuss their feelings helps subdue irrational fears and guilt sentiments associated with thoughts of death. Supporting data come likewise from study of the reactions of people to disaster. They show the need to search for others and for "belongingness" in such situations and the great relief resulting from being able to speak openly and candidly (Bloch, Silber, & Perry, 1956). A psychological shift occurs from attempting to repress and forget to learning to live with the experience.

Our embarrassment at the individual face of death forces the seriously ill and dying person to live alone on the brink of an abyss, with no one to understand him. One is reminded of Tolstoi's Ivan Ilyitch (1904). We do not even permit him to say good-by to us. The results are all too often self-pity, depression, occasionally even psychosis. Our summons is to assist the person to re-create a sense of significant being for himself, whether it be existential, inspirational, or transcendental—to be an individual even though dying.

4. What a person seeks to become may well decide to what he attends in his past. And, yet, how little psychology speaks of the future. Many American psychologists are still trying to fit their phenomena into a Newtonian framework, even after their hero, the physicist, has long since become involved with non-Newtonian concepts (MacLeod, 1957). If psychology is to include the full behavior of man, it must encompass purposive strivings, goals, the meaning of the future. Hardly a contemporary clinical-psychologic explanatory system exists which dares ignore emphasis on the whole person. Nevertheless, weighty geneticism and a myopic stimulus-equivalence response outlook concerning post-maturational changes dominate most of them. Yet, we all realize that what death, love, family, and religion can mean to us at ages twenty, forty, sixty, and eighty may be qualitatively quite different.

Even when death is regarded, it is observed essentially as a static end-point. It is revealing how we accentuate the sharp discontinuity here, but disown it in conceptualizing stimulus and response, the psychologic continuity between child and adult, health and mental illness. Death attitudes are usually viewed as manifestations of a more ultimate reality. Too often is anxiety about death interpreted essentially as a derivative event. Too frequently do we occupy ourselves with the symbolic, as distinct from the "real," aspects of death. Any personality theory worth its salt must make meaningful place for the entire continuum of human existence. Part of our failure to do this, in addition to methodological difficulties, lies in our penchant for externals, geneticism, and the reactive organism model (Allport, 1955). A maximally generative theory will emerge only when we enlarge our view of personality development from a past-up-to-now outlook to admit a from-here-on-into-the-future one also. Truth resides not only in Locke and Hume, but in Leibniz and Brentano as well.

5. Doing research in the world is not quite the same as in the university or research laboratory. We bear responsibility for feeding back to our graduate schools the experiences related here. They underscore the outlook of the 1958 Estes Park conference of the Education and Training Board of the APA (1959) that a large disparity exists between the manner in which much research is effected in the outside world and the formal picture typically presented to the graduate student—a representation which often functions as a basis for decisions concerning the character of the training given students. All too frequently, we stereotype from the finished product rather than from the process-core of the research endeavor. Education for research must develop more than informed powers of mind. It must transmit a sense of potency about coping that can cut across barriers of time and circumstance (Bruner, 1960).

6. I relearned the lesson never to underestimate the power of your own example and tenacity to set others in compassionate motion. It was Andrew Jackson who said, "One man with courage makes a majority"—well, at least sometimes. I also rediscovered that, more often than not, progress proceeds from elusive but vital fractions. There is a relevant saying from the "Pirke Aboth," ("Ethics of the Fathers") of the Talmud: "It is not thy duty to complete the work, but neither art thou free to desist from it."

7. Now, I may be demonstrating my own opinionatedness. It strikes me that the fields of scrutiny represented by our contributors signal that our task is to study "what is, not what is immediately convenient" (Allport, 1960b). All the contributors exhibit the capacity for direct contact with vital experiences and real issues of human being and becoming. Their achievements underline the reality that, even when investigating highly sensitive, "living-tissue" areas, ingenuity, vigor, and courage can suc-

cessfully brush aside curtains of silence. Their work clarifies and intensifies our image of man and his world.

■ Selected Bibliography ■

Allport, G. *Becoming: Basic considerations for a psychology of personality.* New Haven: Yale University Press, 1955.

Allport, G. Religion and adolescence. In *Religion in the developing personality,* Proceedings of the second academy symposium, Academy of Religion and Mental Health. New York: New York University Press, 1960. (a)

Allport, G. The open system in personality theory. *J. abnorm. soc. Psychol.,* 1960, **61**, 301–309. (b)

Bloch, D.A., Silber, E., & Perry, S.E. Some factors in emotional reactions of children to disaster. *Amer. J. Psychiat.,* 1956, **113**, 416–422.

Bottome, Phyllis. *Alfred Adler, a biography.* New York: Putnam, 1939.

Bruner, J.S. *The process of education.* Cambridge: Harvard University Press, 1960.

Education and Training Board of the American Psychological Association. Education for research in psychology. *Amer. Psychol.,* 1959, **14**, 167–179.

Faunce, W.A., & Fulton, R.L. The sociology of death. *Social Forces,* 1958, **36**, 205–209.

Feifel, H. Ego structure and mental deterioration. *J. Pers.,* 1951, **20**, 188–198.

Feifel, H. Attitudes of mentally ill patients toward death. *J. nerv. ment. Dis.,* 1955, **122**, 375–380.

Feifel, H. Judgment of time in younger and older persons. *J. Geront.,* 1957, **12**, 71–75.

Feifel, H. (Ed.) *The meaning of death.* New York: McGraw-Hill, 1959.

Feifel, H. Attitudes toward death in older persons: A symposium. *J. Geront.,* 1961, **16**, 44–66. (a)

Feifel, H. Death–relevant variable in psychology. In R. May (Ed.), *Existential psychology.* New York: Random House, 1961. (b)

Freud, S. Thoughts for the times on war and death. In *Collected papers*. London: Hogarth Press, 1925. Vol. 4.

Fulton, R.L. Attitudes toward death in older persons: A symposium. *J. Geront.*, 1961, 16, 44–66.

Kasper, A.M. The doctor and death. In H. Feifel (Ed.), *The meaning of death*. New York: McGraw-Hill, 1959.

Lydgate, J. Where is thy sting? *Spectator*, 1961, 206, 308.

MacLeod, R.B. Teleology and theory of human behavior. *Science*, 1957, 125, 477–480.

Morgenthau, H.J. Death in the nuclear age. *Commentary*, 1961, 32, 231–234.

Norbeck, E. *Religion in primitive society*. New York: Harper & Brothers, 1961.

Tolstoi, L.N. The death of Ivan Ilyitch. In *The works of Lyof N. Tolstoi*. New York: Charles Scribner's Sons, 1904. Vol. 14.

Wallace, A.C. Human behavior in extreme situations. National Academy of Sciences—National Research Council Publication No. 390. Disaster Study No. 1. Washington, D.C.: 1956.

• 3 •

Human Sexual Behavior

Wardell B. Pomeroy

As an undergraduate thirty years ago, I was warned by my psychology professors that there were two areas of study that were fraught with danger. One was the study of hypnosis, and the second was the study of human sexual behavior. Further inquiry as to why these areas of research were dangerous was met with frosty stares, much harrumphing, and evasion. Dismissal of researchers in at least two psychology departments in the early 1930's because of studies on human sexual behavior could not help but increase the anxiety of psychologists contemplating work in this field. Despite Freud and his followers, Havelock Ellis, German sexologists, and others, only five psychologists had published anything approaching good statistical data on human sexual behavior prior to 1940.

Considering this history of timidity and fearfulness on the part of psychologists, it is little wonder that in 1942 I delayed for six months before deciding to join the staff of the Institute for Sex Research. For the past nineteen years, I have rejoiced in having ignored the advice of my venerated psychology professors. However, although the research has been rewarding in many ways, there have been certain problems connected with it. Some of these are peculiar to any investigation in taboo areas; others are unique to a study of human sexual behavior.

Research workers in all areas have the problem of finding financial support. Salaries must be paid, equipment and supplies must be purchased, travel expenses must be covered. Limited research is sometimes paid for by universities and colleges, but researchers have increasingly become the recipients of grants from private foundations and the government. The financial support of studies of human sex behavior has become more available in the past few years, thanks to less hypocrisy and a more realistic approach to understanding the human animal as a sexual being. Three, and even two, decades ago, however, the situation was different. Thanks to an enlightened Indiana University, to the Committee for Research in Problems of Sex of the National Research Council, and to a public which bought our publications in large numbers, our own research program was able to survive. More recently, the National Institute of Mental Health has supported the Institute for Sex Research on a very adequate scale. The financing of research on human sexual behavior is not now a major problem, but there are other problems that must be solved.

One of these is the problem of sampling. We became aware, very early in the research, of the negative correlation between randomness of the sample and cooperation in giving a sex history. Persons who volunteer to give their histories will be more cooperative than persons who are preselected and then asked to give histories.

To compromise these two antagonistic factors, we have used a group sampling plan whenever possible. By this method, all the members of a functioning social group (for example, fraternities, classrooms, Parent-Teacher Associations, factories, church groups, and the like) are interviewed. At the start, some individual members of these groups are volunteers, and, as the interviewing progresses, others give histories under pressures built up by those who have already been interviewed. A third of our eighteen thousand histories have come from groups in which 100 per cent have cooperated; about one-half have come from groups in which more than three-quarters of the members have given histories. At lower social levels, where group membership is not usual, other techniques, such as sampling from hospitals and hiring halls, have been used. In prisons, where a captive population is available, random probability sampling has been used with refusal rates rarely going above 5 per cent.

Thus far, this has appeared to be the best technique available, but it is possible that, with our changing mores, a random probability sample in the noninstitutional population can be used. At present, we are debating whether to undertake a pilot study testing the feasibility of this type of sampling. Further sampling problems arise when one is investigating some particular aspect of sexual behavior. In our study on sex offenders, now being written, it was possible to secure a sample from the court and prison records of sex offenders, but for a later planned volume on transvestitism it will take a good deal of sleuthing even to know who the transvestites are and a considerable degree of persuasion to secure their cooperation once they are found.

Observation is one of the cornerstones on which the whole scientific process is based. Without repeated, measured observations, we would be in a pre-Wundtian era of psychology. However, our Christian and Talmudic heritage being what it is, the opportunities to make observations and measurements in the study of human sexual behavior are indeed limited. Hence, other techniques, chiefly the interview, have developed. A breakthrough in certain physiological measurements of human sexual behavior is in process by other investigators, but we have always recognized the lacunae caused by our mores as a serious problem in our chosen field. That we have been able to observe and film sexual behavior in other mammals has been helpful in our understanding of human sexual behavior, but it can be useful in only a limited way.

Interviewing in the taboo area of sex behavior has been an intriguing and kaleidoscopic experience. When subjects are convinced that the record they give will be kept confidential and when they perceive that no moral or ethical evaluation is made by the interviewer, they are remarkably cooperative in detailing their own sexual behavior, even though it may put them in an unfavorable light, be illegal, or be contrary to established mores. However, it is clear that the problems of communicating with a wide variety of people who use widely differing sexual and nonsexual vocabularies are much greater in our field than in most areas of research. The drug addicts have their own argot; we must know not only this argot but also those of such groups as the prostitute, the criminal, the homosexual, the lower-level Negro, and the beatnik. A respondent might say; "You see, dis guy was high on tea and Benny, so the spade took out his Lady from Bristol and made a mark"; or: "I like to cruise T-rooms, but lace curtains through a glory hole make me sick." Such a respondent will be reluctant to continue his cooperation if he feels the interviewer is not understanding his vocabulary and hence is not understanding *him*.

Perhaps the most difficult part of our interviewing technique for me to learn was the need for controlling the interview. In the limited amount of training I had had as a clinical psychologist, I was taught that "the customer is always right." This may be good practice in therapy, but it can be disastrous when one is attempting to extract accurate information from a respondent. There are many cross-checks in the history itself that give us information on the veracity of the respondent. Also, hesitations, blushing, uneasiness, and changes of topic may give us clues to possible falsification. For example, we ask about a dozen questions indirectly related to a person's homosexual history before we come to the direct question: "How old were you the first time you had sexual contact with another person of your own sex?" By this time, we are fairly certain whether or not the person has had extensive homosexual experience. If at this point he denies an overt history of homosexuality but there were enough indicators in a positive direction to make us reasonably certain he is covering up, we have learned to refuse to accept his denials. At this stage it becomes necessary to say with firmness, even vehemence, and yet with kindness: "Look, I don't give a damn what you've done, but if you don't tell me the straight of it, it's better that we stop this history right here. Now, how old were you the first time this or that happened [or how often did you do it, or how many partners were there]?" Surprisingly enough, in not a single case has a person refused to continue at this point. In fact, in the eighteen thousand histories we have taken, fewer than ten persons have refused to complete a history once they have started. Of the few who have, most were among those interviewed in the early years of the research when our interviewing techniques were less developed and we were less perceptive as to some of the sensitive areas in the interview.

We have also had to learn when to vary the sequence of questions as well as the way in which the questions are asked, depending on the social level and the particular values that the respondent is expected to have. For example, asking a female about her history of prostitution usually comes near the end of the interview, but a professional prostitute is usually willing to divulge that part of her life much more readily than sexual details of her personal life.

It has been necessary to record in code in order to preserve confidence and also in order to record rapidly so that we do not interfere with the interviewing process. Long pauses during an interview while the researcher is recording what the respondent has just said can seriously interfere with the pace of the interview and hence adversely affect rapport. Since it takes about three months of intensive work to learn this code and another six months of practice to use it with ease, it can be appreciated that training our interviewers in the necessary skills is not a simple matter.

The selection of personnel has been one of the major problems in our research. This is particularly true for the position of interviewer. Unlike most research projects, where the interviewers are typically at a lower echelon in the organization, we believe that the most sophisticated statistical treatment available will not make bad data into good. Hence, each person who takes case histories is a trustee of the Institute for Sex Research and is a member of the policy-making board. Over a period of twenty-two years, nearly three hundred persons have been considered as possible interviewers, from which a total of nine have been selected. The problems in selecting personnel in this sensitive area have been considerable and can best be summarized by pointing out three almost paradoxical requirements.

First, we prefer someone who is happily married, since never-married persons who investigate human sexual behavior are suspect by many persons in our culture. On the other hand, we need someone who is able to travel extensively. Second, the person must be well trained in some area of science and yet must be able to gain rapport and actually enjoy working with people of lower socioeconomic groups. It is rare in the pursuit of higher learning that the lines to the common man are left uncut. Ivory towers may be quiet hideaways to facilitate cerebration, but they are unsuitable for learning "the facts of life." I remember Karl Lashley once remarking that very few psychologists really liked people, and I am inclined to agree there is a certain amount of truth in this observation. Third, it is important for a sex research worker to have lived in our culture, speak our language, be fully aware of our Puritan heritage, and yet be so unaffected by it that he has no moral evaluation, as a scientist, about what other people do sexually. Obviously, this can never be completely accomplished. However, there are few areas of research in which the investigator's own system of morals is so challenged and are so crucial as in the study of human sexual behavior.

There are also other factors that must be considered when selecting personnel for a study of sex behavior. One applicant for a job with us fulfilled the above-mentioned desiderata, but his wife was an alcoholic and completely untrustworthy. Another applicant would have been hired except that he had been so active in antireligious, antisegregationist, and prounion activities that his presence on our staff would have been a constant source of difficulty in securing cooperation in many quarters. We

27

must avoid hiring anyone who is identified with either ultra-radical or ultraconservative movements or institutions. Although we have our own opinions and attitudes concerning social issues, we have learned that we must not expound them in public.

It has been suggested that we have women interviewers to interview women, and Negro interviewers to interview Negroes. No one has yet suggested we have prostitutes to interview prostitutes or drug addicts to interview drug addicts, although it would seem that the same logic might operate. It appears to us that the qualities of the interviewer and not his sex, race, or personal history are the important variables. We now have a woman taking case histories, and preliminary calculations indicate that she is getting the same amount and quality of sexual information from male and female respondents as are the three male interviewers.

Even with the less highly skilled jobs, it is necessary to secure persons who are completely trustworthy, mature, and stable. They cannot be offended by the type of material with which we deal and must view it objectively and calmly. Such personnel are at a premium and must be paid more than the ordinary person filling such jobs as secretary, statistical calculator, translator, or librarian. Even janitorial service becomes a problem, because of security restrictions. (In twenty-three years, we have had a change of janitors only twice.) A few weeks ago, when our current janitor had to retire because of age, failing vision, and general decrepitude, we spent a considerable amount of time and energy with security checks before we felt we were ready to entrust the "night key" to our third janitor. It might be added that we also are not able to use the ordinary student help that lightens the load (and sometimes even carries it) in many research projects.

In our field of research, the problem of the legal status of the study and of the researcher is an important one. In the first place, our sex laws are so out of step with what people do sexually that more than 90 per cent of all the men and more than 80 per cent of all the women in the country could have been sent to prison for what they have done sexually. We have considered the data obtained in our interviews as communications. Lawyers, doctors, and the clergy have been shielded from disclosing privileged communications, but to my knowledge the rights of the researcher have never been tested in the courts. Although several lawyers have assured us that our position could be upheld, until such a test is made there will always remain a doubt. Some years ago, the United States Customs Department seized several shipments of erotic books, pictures, and objects sent us from abroad, claiming that it was illegal for us to receive such material. It took us seven years and a good many thousands of dollars in legal fees to win this battle. Fortunately, the decision on the case was unequivocally in favor of the right of scientists to have access to such material for study and analysis. There are few, if any, other areas in the behavioral sciences where greater risks and greater care are necessary in scientific exploration.

Another problem we face is that of public relations. Because human sexual behavior is such an emotionally charged subject, any study of it brings a much greater public reaction and much more newspaper and magazine publicity than a comparable study in an area of lesser affect. In 1953, more than one hundred fifty magazines and newspapers asked to review our volume on the female before it was released to the public. We selected about thirty of those we considered the most reputable and provided them with prepublication galley proofs. We had hoped in this fashion to reduce and control the publicity attendant on the publication of the book. This system did, in fact, reduce the amount of publicity at that time and also ensured a more responsible presentation to the public. But the impact of the simultaneous reviews by the thirty magazines was such that it gave a somewhat different impression to the general reading public. Thus, we have been criticized for seeking publicity. We have, however, suffered as a result of the publicity attendant on our research and have actually sought to reduce it. In 1958, for our last publication, *Pregnancy, Birth, and Abortion,* in a further effort to control irresponsible statements to the public, we allowed only one magazine prepublication rights. I am certain that there will be some who will interpret this article as an effort to secure more publicity. Companies have attempted to use our name (and especially the name of Kinsey) to advertise products such as phonograph records, sex manuals, and articles of clothing—specifically brassières—and have also tried to buy the movie rights to the volumes on the male and female.

There have been more than thirty books (probably as many as fifty) that have been commentaries on or summaries of *Sexual Behavior in the Human Male* and/or *Sexual Behavior in the Human Female*. At first blush, this might seem complimentary, and in a sense it is. However, in some of these books there are many misrepresentations of our research and misreporting of specific data, and in most of the books there are at least a few such examples of inaccurate reporting. Innumerable times, people have reported to us that they have read our reports in paperback, which means only that they have read some condensation of, or commentary on, our research. They often then report a statement attributed to us which we did not make and which is either wrong or judgmental. A majority of persons (even including many scientists) have erroneously assumed that we have authorized such publications, and the mistakes in them are being forever laid at our doorstep. The inevitable errors that we ourselves have made in our own publications are enough without having to bear the burden of the mistakes of others.

Another type of publication has arisen and proliferated—novels concerning sex researchers. The prototype was published and quickly reached the best-seller list two years ago, and already there are at least a dozen such novels on the market. The authors usually disclaim any connection to us (thus avoiding libel action), but the inevitable comparisons with our research are made. It is difficult to think of another research project in any area which has been subjected to this type of misrepresentation and harassment.

As mentioned earlier, previous studies in this area were thwarted for one reason or another by the taboo surrounding sex in our culture. One excellent study was completed and then locked away and has to this day never been released. In most research programs, there has been a sound body of scientific knowledge that has served as a background and foundation for further research. In our own particular area, we have been handicapped by the paucity of information based on careful and controlled studies and at the same time have been overwhelmed by the amount of conjecture, moralizing, and wishful thinking that the literature provides.

However, with the climate changing in the direction of a more relaxed attitude toward investigation and discussion of sexual behavior, we can reasonably anticipate an increase in the quantity and quality of research on sex. Interestingly enough, progress feeds on progress. For example, our own publications of thirteen and eight years ago have now opened doors to us that might otherwise have been closed.

One intriguing problem that appears to be exacerbated in this area of research is its attraction to a large lunatic fringe of pseudoscientists. All disciplines have a certain number of these people, many of whom are neurotic or even psychotic, who dabble in what they consider research and who tell ". . . tale[s]/ . . . , full of sound and fury,/ Signifying nothing." I have listened to more crackpot ideas with overtones of astrology, phrenology, electricity, magnetism, and pure fantasy than the average psychiatrist in a mental hospital encounters in many years of work. Ph.D.'s and M.D.'s are not excluded from this group, and it sometimes takes a considerable degree of tact to let such a crackpot down politely and gently.

Another problem, tangential to our research, has been the number of impostors who use our name to serve their own ends. We receive about a dozen letters a year from all parts of the country asking if we have an interviewer working in such-and-such a community taking interviews by phone. We offer our aid in bringing such persons to justice, but they are rarely apprehended.

If this paper resembles a wailing wall for all the trials of the poor sex researcher, let me hasten to deny this. The added problems that our subject matter entails have made the quest for knowledge in this area that much more exciting, and I would not trade places with the rat psychologist for all the T-mazes and Skinner boxes in the world.

▪ Selected Bibliography ▪

Amer. J. Sociol. 1956, 62,, (2). (The entire volume is on interviewing.)

Bandura, A., & Walters, R.H. *Adolescent aggression.* New York: Ronald Press, 1959.

Gebhard, P.H., Pomeroy, W.B., Martin, C.E., & Christenson, Cornelia V. *Pregnancy, birth, and abortion.* New York: Harper Brothers and Paul B. Hoeber, 1958.

Grazia, S. de. *Errors of psychotherapy.* Garden City, New York: Doubleday & Company, 1952.

Himelhoch, J., & Fava, Sylvia F. (Eds.) *Sexual behavior in American society; An appraisal of the first two Kinsey reports.* New York: W.W. Norton, 1955.

Hyman, H.H., et al. *Interviewing in social research.* Chicago: University of Chicago Press, 1954.

Kahn, R.L., & Cannell, C.F. *The dynamics of interviewing: Theory, technique, and cases.* New York: John Wiley, 1957.

Kinsey, A.C., Pomeroy, W.B., & Martin, C.E. *Sexual behavior in the human male.* Philadelphia: W.B. Saunders, 1948.

Kinsey, A.C., Pomeroy, W.B., Martin, C.E., & Gebhard, P.H. *Sexual behavior in the human female.* Philadelphia: W.B. Saunders, 1953.

▪ 4 ▪

Suicide

Edwin S. Shneidman

The history of suicide reveals that it has been viewed with varying attitudes by society.[1] Some primitive and some recent cultures have accepted and approved of suicide. But by far the most prevalent attitude, especially in Occidental cultures, has been negative, and suicidal behavior has been met with hostility, censure, and condemnation. Suicide falls directly in the middle of a taboo area and thus encounters all the blind prejudices and resistances which encrust proscribed topics. As Glanville Williams (1957) remarks: ". . . It raises the marital disputes of order and freedom, effort and indulgence, holiness and happiness, authority and conscience, which have vexed philosophy for as

[1] This paper grows from experiences of a larger study, supported by USPHS Mental Health Project Grant OM-128 from the National Institute of Mental Health, United States Public Health Service. Edwin S. Shneidman and Norman L. Farberow are co-project directors.

long as these problems have been thought of, and are unable to achieve any permanent solution" (p. 248).

Taboos generally involve various kinds of activities which are forbidden. For example, there are (1) things which one would not do (the taboo is on the action); (2) things which one does with relative impunity, if not enjoyment, but would not talk about having done (the taboo is on the discussion); and (3) activities which one would not even dare to do or even wish to think of (the taboo is on the thought or label). Suicide seems to cut across all three kinds of taboo; the prohibitions against suicide (and murder) may be found more often in the first (action) and third (thought) kinds of taboo, whereas the topics of heterosexuality and homosexuality may be found more in the second (discussion) type of taboo.

Each of the topics in this volume is taboo; yet, without indulging in any competition as to which topic is *most* taboo, it can be said that suicide shares taboos with each of the major areas in a kind of overlapping which is not necessarily reciprocal. For example, the overlap of the taboos of suicide with those relating to death, sex, and the hereafter may be presented briefly.

The relationships between death and suicide would appear obvious, but turn out to be, on examination, somewhat complicated. True, committing suicide involves death, but the act of committing suicide can also be conceived as a way of living (or non-living). The taboos relating to death are discussed elsewhere in this volume and need not be detailed here except briefly.

Death is reified and reacted to in many ways. A recent Radcliffe dissertation (Greenberger, 1961) has helpfully outlined some attitudes on the meaning of death. She lists the following: death as *unreal* (". . . the difficulty or impossibility of accepting one's own death. Because we are reluctant to die, the concept of immortality always has been enticing to man . . ."); death as *punishment* (". . . death as punishment for forbidden [tabooed] wishes . . ."); death as *separation,* especially from the mother or parents; death as *reunion,* especially with the mother or the incestuous love object; and death as *lover.* (The literature on this last point is an extensive and fascinating one and is discussed by McClelland [1963]). The reader will note the many and rather clear threads of taboo running through this tapestry of death. And suicide, with its dark motivations for immortality, punishment, and reunion, is spun from the same loom.

What are some of the relationships between suicide and sex? Over and above the notions that people seem to commit suicide over unrequited heterosexual love and that some adolescent transvestites as well as some homosexuals commit suicide—it has been reported that homosexuals are disproportionately represented in the suicide population, but we have never seen any good evidence of this—a most interesting concept is that, alluded to above, of death as somehow sexual, as a lover. McClelland (1963) discusses the association of "death, seduction, and demonic power." In women (men were not studied), excitement, sexual fantasies, and upsurge of libidinal energies were found to be associated with death, that is, expressed more often by women dying of cancer than by seriously ill, but not dying, counterparts. In this area, all the taboos about sex, death, and suicide are compounded.

A recent study of ours (Farberow, Shneidman, & Leonard, 1962) on suicide in patients with malignant neoplasms revealed additional relationships between suicide and death. Cancer, as a fatal illness with death lurking in the shadows, arouses feelings of disquiet and displeasure similar to those aroused by suicide. Suicide was viewed paradoxically when it occurred in such patients, often being seen as justifiable and reasonable. Many people, when asked under what conditions suicide would ever be justified, offer the presence of a serious terminal illness as just cause. Yet, even when it did occur among patients with cancer, the familiar feelings of guilt, shame, and embarrassment appeared, not only in members of the family, but also among the hospital staff. Why does a person at the threshold of death commit suicide? Perhaps the value of his life is lessened for the man who knows that he will not live much longer anyway and faces a foreshortened future filled with pain and suffering. The choice of suicide over an existence in which the life pattern has been totally disrupted, the body image attacked, the self-concept severely strained, and all familiar interpersonal relationships practically destroyed seems, on the face of it, understandable.

Yet the number of suicides which occur in cancer patients is only a small percentage of the total number of patients who contract the dread disease. Perhaps the question equally deserving to be asked is why so many cancer patients do not commit suicide. The strength of the taboos against suicide becomes even more remarkable when the attitudes of the physicians toward the dying patient are studied. Feifel, *supra,* and Weisman and Hackett (1962) have described some of the tendencies toward rejection and denial which appear in the physician when faced with the impending death of a patient. Weisman and Hackett say: "The patient's capacity to face his own imminent death is often underestimated, while the doctor's capacity to face the patient's death is usually overestimated. . . . If the doctor can accept death as a fact of life and not as a failure of treatment, he can accept the reality of the dying patient" (p. 19).

Suicide and the hereafter have an intimate, complicated relationship. Among the many notions, two facts can be stated: (1) some people believe in a hereafter, some do not, and some are not sure; (2) belief in a hereafter seems to inhibit suicide in some people and to facilitate it in others. This entire topic is not only a fascinating one, but one which is, to put it strongly, fundamental to more effective understanding of suicidal phenomena and ultimately basic to more effective treatment, control, and prevention of these behaviors.

Tabooed areas are, by definition, socially disapproved, stigmatized, and unpopular. Harold Hildreth, of the United States Public Health Service, has suggested that researches or investigations in taboo areas often have three common characteristics. First, they often deal with fundamental social problems—the types of things that people do not want to recognize or proper people do not want to get involved in. Second, there is some suspicion of investigators in such areas. There is a personal cost in an investigation in a generally taboo area, the least of which is the ubiquitous journalistic question, "How did you come to be interested in this topic?"—with the sly implication that it must be some grossly overdetermined interest or concern on the researcher's part. Third, there are common methodological problems in investigations in taboo areas; for example, the data are characteristically difficult to obtain, and there are pervasive questions of the reliability of the data, in that people tend to dissimulate and conceal.

From the research standpoint, these methodological issues are most important. They lead directly to the problem of the reliability of statistics of suicide. Much of the technical and popular literature on suicide is filled with so-called statistics and norms comparing suicide rates of various races, regions, religions, nationalities, and so on. The question is important in both social and personality theory as to whether these differences do exist or what are the true statistics. It may be of interest to note that the word "statistic" is derived from the Latin *status,* which in the Middle Ages had come to mean a "state" in the political sense of the word. Statistics, therefore, was originally an inquiry into various conditions of the state and has been called "political arithmetic" and, later, "vital statistics." In these early labors, much attention was given to tables of mortality for the state, so that the present discussion of statistics on suicide is, in terms of the original sense of the word, particularly appropriate.

Statistics on suicide come from the individual certifications of individual deaths. These certifications are made by county coroners or medical examiners and are then compiled by state, region, and nation. Differing procedures, however, are followed in other countries, so that some certifications are made on the recommendation of the local or family physician only. Assuming an omniscient power privy to the real nature of each death, any departure from the tabulations by such a power would represent a distortion in the statistics. These errors in statistics on suicide occur for one of the following reasons: (1) There are inadvertent errors of diagnosis (for example, calling a suicidal death an accidental death) where there are no taboos influencing the diagnostician. (2) There are deliberate or unconscious suppressions of the diagnosis for reasons related to taboo.

Coroners certify each death as homicide, natural, accident, or suicide. This is often difficult simply because the *mode* of death is not readily apparent. For example, a woman can be found dead, and the coroner's ancillary people—the toxicologist, the histologist, the biochemist, and so on—can tell him rather exactly what the distribution of a barely lethal dosage of barbiturate is among the organs in her body, but this may give little information as to whether the death was accidental or suicidal. The *sine qua non* of suicide is some lethal self-destructive intention, so what is missing from the coroner's information is the victim's motivation or intention; and these are psychological concepts. In Los Angeles County, the professional members of the Suicide Prevention Center, sponsored by the Public Health Service, have been deputized by Chief Medical Examiner-Coroner Theodore Curphey to serve as his "suicide team." We do "psychological autopsies," interviewing, in cases of equivocal accident-suicide deaths, the relatives and friends of the deceased; reconstructing the life style of the victim; searching for undiagnosed depressions, psychoses, and personality changes; and keeping our ears attuned for coded messages of suicidal intent which may have been dropped by the victim into the matrix of communication. It may be added that these interviews with the survivors have a generally therapeutic effect, just in relieving some of their taboo feelings. As a result of these activities, two conclusions emerge.

(1) The existing fourfold classification of deaths into homicide, accident, natural, and suicide is oversimplified and often leads to inaccuracy. Consider the following: death by invasion of an unwelcome bullet or windshield is called accidental, but death by invasion of an unwelcome virus is called natural. We speak of cerebral-vascular accidents, but are they not really cerebral-vascular "naturals"? Shooting oneself to death is called suicide, but drinking oneself to death is called natural. Provoking a spouse or bandit to kill one is called homicide; provoking an animal to kill one is called accident. It is too confusing, primarily because the psychological factors—the individual's intentions, his motivations, and his role in his own demise—are omitted. What

is suggested is a psychologically oriented classification of death phenomena focused on the individual's role in his own demise (Shneidman, 1963).

Thus it may well be that few of the statistics on suicide in the world (with the possible exception of those stemming from Los Angeles County) can be deemed reliable. Certifications of obviously suicidal deaths as natural deaths or accidental deaths by physicians and coroners often occur in rural and urban areas throughout the world. "Suicide" is a dirty word. Indeed, some languages have no word for suicide. Mussolini made it illegal, and thus there are no statistics on suicide in Italy for part of that period. In one of our studies (Shneidman & Farberow, 1960), we compared, using a blind analysis approach, the psychological content of 948 suicide notes from Los Angeles County for the years 1956 through 1958 with a set of socioeconomic variables determined by the area in which the note-writer lived and found that the taboos relating to the method and meaning of suicide varied among the socioeconomic levels. Conscientious coroners must be making arbitrary decisions daily concerning the mode of death which they put on the death certificate.

(2) Relatively few individuals who kill themselves do so unambivalently. Granted that some suicidal behaviors have no lethal intention, we believe that most suicidal behavior involves a gamble with death, magical thinking, or dependence on the role of the significant other in a dyadic relationship and is acutely ambivalent.

The taboo nature of suicide apparently does not prevent its discussion. The taboo seems to accrue much more to the act than to the writing about the topic. The bibliography on suicide printed in *The Cry for Help* (Farberow & Shneidman, 1961) covering the years from 1897, the date of Durkheim's book, to 1957 contains about two thousand titles,—although it is fair to state that most of the items are discursive, philosophic, anecdotal, or theoretical in nature, and few have scientific substance.

The taboo which emerges in the hostility of society toward suicidal acts also seems to vary according to the type of act. There is a great onus attached to surviving spouse, parent, or child of a suicide. No other kind of death—whether by accident, cancer, or heart disease—creates such a backwash of guilt, remorse, and shame. Open hostility, on the other hand, is often reserved, not for the person who commits suicide, but for the person who, to use a word in an un-American way, "unsuccessfully" attempts it. We have heard reports of emergency hospital personnel saying: "Next time, really do a good job and don't bother us." It may well be that these feelings are directed toward the person for his daring to do the tabooed thing, to show disdain for society and its values and disregard of the religious strictures. In addition, some of this anger may be directed toward the individual for his semantic usurpation, that is, his indulging in *nonlethal* "suicide" behavior.

One example illustrating most of the points mentioned above occurred when the Los Angeles medical examiner-coroner received petitions from the family and friends of a man who had obviously committed suicide indicating that the deceased was a fine citizen and a good husband and father; when the coroner did not change the certification of mode of death, the widow sued him. The judge ruled that the medical examiner-coroner, using his own judgment and the services of our group, had shown diligence and care, and the plaintiff's case was denied. At this point, the woman became assaultive and hysterical. Rarely was the taboo nature of suicide more dramatically portrayed.

Consider another illustration of the taboo nature of this topic. Some months ago, one of us had occasion to conduct a workshop on suicide prevention in a large city and was contacted by a member of a well-known religious group interested in suicide prevention. This member indicated that he was going to visit and counsel a young man who had recently attempted suicide and extended an invitation to accompany him. Four hours were spent in the home with the young man and his wife. One of several interesting developments was that the suicide attempt was never mentioned, although the topic of sex and specific sexual behaviors was unabashedly introduced by the clergyman and answered with seeming candor and lack of resentment by the young couple. The taboo word in that context was "suicide," although that was the *raison d'être* of the meeting. It might be added that we do things somewhat differently at the Suicide Prevention Center. There is the apocryphal story that, when Kinsey died, a publisher indicated to Kinsey's group that he would like to publish their materials because, as he said, for him, " 'Sex' was not a four-letter word." For us, using the same kind of arithmetic, "suicide" is not a four-letter word either.

A final example of the effect of taboos on suicide statistics can be given. The sheriff-coroner of a large city once showed us some data on suicide in his city which were remarkable, for he had noted only a dozen suicidal deaths annually for a city of over one-half million. We looked at his records with some interest and discovered that he was reporting as suicide only those deaths in which he found a verified, holographic suicide note. In those cases in which the individual seemed to have killed himself but did not leave a note, the case was not reported as suicide, but as "self-inflicted violent deaths," and recorded as accident.

There seems to be some slight change toward the lifting of the taboo nature of suicide, just as there have been great changes in the taboo nature of sex. For example, the status of suicide as a crime has been changing. State after state has taken it off the statute books. In only three states—New Jersey, North Dakota, and South Dakota—is attempted suicide a crime. As recently as 1961, in California, suicide was not a compensable industrial injury case. Now, if the suicide was precipitated by pain or mental anguish derived from the industrial accident, it may be compensable.

Taboo is such a generally negative concept that it is appropriate to ask a perverse question, namely: Are there any positive aspects to taboo? Are any taboos worthwhile and effective? In some taboos, especially in the sexual area, their purpose is obviously to perpetuate some ideal that society deems worthwhile. However, in other areas, taboos seem to operate against the goals of society. Thus, our information does not lead us to believe that taboos against suicide lead to any decrease in suicide rate. Indeed, quite the contrary seems to be true. (It is important to report that, on the other side, our activity has not led us to believe that research and study of suicide increase the suicide rate.) It must not be assumed that it is our wish to lift all taboos. What so often happens, however, is that the taboos are directed not only against the act but against the investigation and investigators of the act as well. We are against suicide; we seek principles which can effect a reduction in the suicide rate. But, being against the phenomena means that we must break through the barrier surrounding the taboo and attempt, contrary to the taboo, to promote investigation of the subject.

In addition, we can ask if there is anything positive for investigators in a taboo area. Though there is obvious onus attached to investigating taboo topics, there are subtle rewards as well. Whereas we are seen by some as brash, we are seen by others as courageous. The approbation of many comes out in their being pleased that we are working in this taboo topic. This helps in the current mitigation of the taboo indicated above. Our problem is how to explain to the psychological conservatives our radical challenging of some of the unconscious primitive roots of the society. Our intuitive explanation is that we are living in a rapidly changing world and that, because of this, we must have the courage to investigate the magical, irrational, and overfeared inhabitants relegated to the cellar of our societal edifice.

Aside from the taboo nature of suicide, if we have learned anything from our decade of work on this topic, we have learned that, happily, most individuals who are acutely suicidal are so for only a relatively short period and that, even during the time they are suicidal, they are extremely ambivalent about living and dying. If there are techniques for identifying these individuals before rash acts are taken and if there are agencies, like the Suicide Prevention Center, in the community that can throw in every resource on the side of life and give the individual some temporary surcease or sanctuary, then after a short time most individuals can go on, voluntarily and willingly, to live useful and creative lives.

■ Selected Bibliography ■

Farberow, N.L., Shneidman, E.S. (Eds.) *The cry for help*. New York: McGraw-Hill, 1961.

Farberow, N.L., Shneidman, E.S., & Leonard, Calista V. Suicide among general medical and surgical patients with malignant neoplasms. *VA med. Bull.*, Feb., 1963.

Greenberger, Ellen S. *Fantasies of women confronting death: A study of critically ill patients*. Unpublished dissertation, Radcliffe College, 1961.

McClelland, D.C. The Harlequin complex. In R.W. White (Ed.), *The study of lives*. New York: Atherton Press, 1963. Pp. 94–119.

Shneidman, E.S., & Farberow, N.L. (Eds.) *Clues to suicide*. New York: McGraw-Hill, 1957.

Shneidman, E.S., & Farberow, N.L. A sociopsychological investigation of suicide. In H.E. David & J.C. Brengelman (Eds.) *Perspectives in personality research*. New York: Springer, 1960.

Shneidman, E.S. Orientations toward death: A vital aspect of the study of lives. In R.W. White (Ed.), *The study of lives*. New York: Atherton Press, 1963. Pp. 200–227.

Weisman, A.D., & Hackett, T.P. The dying patient. *Forest Hosp. Publ.* [Des Plaines, Ill.], 1962, 1, 16–21.

▪ 5 ▪

Male Homosexuality

Evelyn Hooker

The inclusion of the topic "male homosexuality" in this volume may suggest that problems of unusual difficulty are associated with research in the area.[1] Although the behavior in question is subject to strong prohibitions enforced by legal and other mechanisms of social control, or taboos, this does not in itself create a taboo on research inquiry. That it creates problems for the investigator is self-evident, but these problems are in no sense unique to the problem area. To treat them as unique or as special to the tabooed area of research is to obscure the real issue. That issue is the same, irrespective of the content of the research, whether it be the DNA code in genetics or male homosexuality—the difficulty of developing good theoretical formula-

[1] This investigation was supported by Research Grants M-839 and M-6452 and a Research Career Award from the National Institute of Mental Health of the National Institutes of Health, Public Health Service.

tions of significant problems which can be tested by appropriate data or of utilizing the data in such a way as to generate new theoretical formulations. Research on male homosexuality is difficult for precisely the same reasons that all other scientific inquiry is difficult: it requires all the ingenuity and resourcefulness of the investigator, all of his capacity for disciplined work, and maximum objectivity.

An examination of some of the problems encountered in the course of a sustained research inquiry may demonstrate the validity of this. The research began with a relatively simple design—to compare a group of adult, male, overt homosexuals who were not seeking therapy for homosexuality or other problems and who were able to manage a viable way of life with a group of heterosexual males who met the same criteria in order to determine whether particular patterns of personality organization characterized a particular psychosexual object choice. In the course of the interviews with the homosexual men, it became clear that the essential features of personality organization could not be understood apart from the social setting in which they were functioning, so that the scope of the research was extended to the total homosexual community. Perhaps a more accurate way of describing the sequence is to say that the social patterns of the research subjects, about which I had been asking questions from the beginning, inevitably led me to an interest in the homosexual community, or "world," as a form of social organization and to the important theoretical question of the relation between personality and social organization.

The first problems were finding research subjects and securing their cooperation. The standard sources of supply—clinics, mental hospitals, and prisons—could not be used because of the criteria for the selection of the sample. The other potential sources were homosexual organizations (which had recently been formed in the community in which the research was to be undertaken), informal social groups of friends and acquaintances, and such known gathering places for homosexual contacts as bars. Having made a pilot study of an informal group of friends at their invitation shortly before beginning the research project, I had a working knowledge of the special language, the general "round of life," and the areas of concern and concealment. Perhaps most important, I had found that direct, genuine ways of establishing relationships with persons whose patterns of behavior differ from one's own were as effective in producing cooperation in this group as in any other. Although my original access to a group of research subjects had been by chance and had, in part, made it easier to establish a research contact with homosexual organizations, there is every reason to believe that today any qualified research worker could secure the initial cooperation of potential research subjects from any one or all of the three sources.

In asserting that locating potential sources of subjects and securing their cooperation does not involve unusual difficulties I am making some assumptions about the qualifications of the investigator which should be made explicit. In addition to the usual prerequisites of training in the social sciences and experience in field work which involves working with persons whose social patterns differ markedly from his own, he must have developed the capacity to view the behavior of homosexuals and to listen to whatever he hears as simply matters of interest. He must be able to look *with* them at their world. The researcher is not an agent of change; his task is to see "how things are," to understand the phenomenon which he is investigating. Research on preventive or therapeutic aspects of homosexuality might, of course, alter the role of the investigator so that he does become an agent of change. Objectivity, as the prime qualification for any scientific undertaking, is never more needed than in the relationship established with homosexuals and the world in which they live. If the investigator cannot detach himself from the evaluative attitudes of the larger society, on the one hand, or of the homosexual world, on the other, and take a dispassionate, objective view, he cannot succeed in obtaining either the cooperation of research subjects or reliable information about their world. That this is extraordinarily difficult to do, in view of the intensity with which homosexuality is condemned in some sectors of our society, on the one hand, and of the intensity with which some homosexuals view that condemnation, on the other, will be so apparent as to require no documentation. That the objective view is not achieved all at once or that, even having been achieved, it is not constantly maintained, will also be apparent. The struggle is continuous.

To locate sources of research subjects and to establish a co-operative attitude on the part of at least some of the potential subjects is only the beginning. Homosexuals vary a great deal in their willingness to be interviewed, as Leznoff (1956) has described. Some "welcome being interviewed with wild anticipation" (p. 202), whereas others are extremely reluctant or refuse completely. To obtain representative samples of all of the varied sectors of the homosexual world is, therefore, a time-consuming process. Those most eager to be interviewed represent a small segment of the population. The willingness to be interviewed or to give more than superficial information at the outset depends on the ability of the researcher to establish himself in the homosexual world as a person to be trusted. How is this to be accomplished?

For the researcher to be trusted, he must demonstrate repeatedly and over time that he takes professional ethics seriously, that under no circumstances would he reveal to anyone what has been told him in confidence. Verbal assurances that he will not reveal what has been told him and that absolute confidence will be maintained at whatever cost, in resistance to whatever pressure may be exerted, must be given with completely genuine intent. He must be prepared to act on them, because pressures will be exerted. Over time, such assurances will be believed if they are reinforced by evidence gathered by members of the homosexual world that in fact the researcher does not, under any provocation, talk to one person about another. Members of the homosexual world also gather evidence about the researcher's trustworthiness in settings other than homosexual ones, such as public presentations or social gatherings in the wider community in which the homosexual may be present but "passing." The researcher must assume that at all times his attitudes and behavior with respect to the seriousness with which he takes his professional ethics are being scrutinized and tested, whether or not he is aware of it.

To be trusted, the investigator must also be able to demonstrate that he does in fact hear whatever is said and observe whatever happens without evaluation, that he is genuinely interested in knowing the homosexual world as the member knows it, and that his only purpose is to understand. He will be tested by his subjects in many ways. For example, indirect or open suggestions will be made that hidden motives are being served by the research. Such references may characterize the researcher as an agent of law enforcement agencies, as being homosexual himself and unwilling or unable to accept the fact, as a social reformer, or as a writer who is collecting material for a sensational exposé. The assumption is almost universal that no one would engage in research in the area simply for the purpose of scientifically understanding the phenomenon. The genuineness of the researcher's nonjudgmental attitude will also be tested by references to activities about which the subject knows, but "only second hand" and "of course, doesn't engage in himself," and which "of course, would be shocking" to the researcher.

Trust, however, must be established with each new person, and it can never be taken for granted. It is a problem to be solved over and over again, as long as the research continues. For example, some members of the homosexual world who occupied strategic positions with respect to the information about operations of public gathering places were so reluctant to be interviewed that five years elapsed before they were willing to risk the interview. The integrity of the researcher had to be vouched for repeatedly by friends of the person from whom the research interview was sought, social introductions had to be arranged, special conditions had to be met for the circumstances in which the interview was to take place, and the appointment for the interview was made and canceled a number of times before it finally occurred. The "strategic member," or gatekeeper of special kinds of information, is, however, not unusual with respect to such problems. Only by persistent and resourceful effort and solid evidence that trust is not misplaced can every sector of the homosexual world be reached. Since that world consists of overlapping communication networks, the process is a slow one, of following the links from person to person, from clique to clique, and from one social setting to another.

Other problems relate to the researcher's role in the homosexual world. In order both to find individual subjects who meet particular research requirements and to gather data on social activities by direct observation the researcher must participate in a wide variety of those activities. The nature of his participation will not only affect the activities themselves but will, in part, determine the observations he is able to make.

The possibilities and limits of participation for women researchers in the male homosexual world are quite different from those for men. Many of the social gatherings in that world are exclusively male; even when present, women are usually a very small minority. The kind of participation which will permit observation for women researchers depends on age, personal appearance, social skill, and manner. In some sectors of that world, young, attractive professional women who are socially adept and who are "wise" and accepting of the homosexual round-of-life not only have no difficulties in gaining access but are much sought after. In other sectors, they would find admission difficult. The older professional woman who is genuine and skillful and who has the capacity to relate easily to persons from a broad cross-section of social levels may find a different kind of acceptance, as a sexually nonthreatening, benign "mother." (These two descriptions are not meant to exhaust all possible varieties of women research workers in the field!) There are, however, many limitations on the activities which can be directly observed by any woman research worker. These limitations can be in part made up for by intensive interviews about the activities.

No such limitations obviously exist for the male researcher, simply by virtue of his ability, as a function of his gender, to "pass" if he chooses to do so. For many male researchers in our society, however, to be emotionally comfortable "passing" in a male homosexual group is difficult. To behave as a member behaves requires the use of special language and gestures and the ability to handle sexual overtures easily. The taboo on homosexuality in our society creates a difficult role problem for the male researcher. Probably this fact, more than any other, accounts for the assumption that research in the area is taboo.

In spite of these differences, however, many of the issues of participant observation are the same in the area of male homosexuality for both male and female researchers. One issue is whether the investigator should identify himself in his professional role and, if so, when and how. The resolution of this issue depends in part on the duration of the research and its specific character. If the research is to be accomplished in a relatively short period and if intensive individual interviews are not an essential feature of it, it is possible that the professional role of the investigator need not be openly identified. When, however, intensive individual interviews are to be employed as a research method and/or the investigator is engaged in a long-term project in the same community, it is not only impossible to avoid the professional identification, but identification is both necessary and desirable. The problem of trust is so critical that any simulation or evasion may damage the ongoing character of the research. It is true, of course, that in social gatherings knowledge of the research worker's professional interest in homosexuality may produce in the participants self-conscious concern or hostility and change the character of the activities. I have found, however, that the researcher can handle the situation in a straightforward way by describing his basic viewpoint as simply trying to see this world as the member sees it, without evaluation, and by demonstrating that this is indeed the case. The feeling so frequently expressed by the homosexual that he simply wants to be "let alone" and does not want to be looked at as a "guinea pig" will change if he can be helped to realize that he is not being "looked at," but that the researcher is looking *with* him at his world.

Another issue is the manner and degree of participation and involvement. If the viewpoint of the researcher, as already described, is the condition under which trust and cooperation can be achieved, it seems clear that a high degree of involvement with the persons and in the activities is an inevitable corollary.

The researcher who does not enjoy persons, irrespective of sexual pattern, who span a broad spectrum of talent, intelligence, occupation, and personality characteristics and who does not become humanly involved in their aspirations and failures, their tragedies and joys, will discover little beyond surface phenomena in the homosexual world. To become humanly involved in that world increases the difficulty of being objective about it, multiplying the number of calls for assistance in the trouble areas. The probability that the protective layers of concealment can be lifted is, however, heightened. In my experience, there are cycles of participation and involvement, followed by withdrawal and efforts to study the data gathered and to achieve distance from the phenomena.

The problems which we have been examining thus far are ones which arise under the assumption that the research investigator is, at the outset, a comparative stranger to the homosexual world and that to find his way in this world special knowledge and skills are required. The effect of the taboo on open and public discussion of any feature of this hidden group except the most sensational and sordid ones is, generally speaking, to create a kind of mystique about how such knowledge and skills can be achieved. I hope that I have given some documentation of the fact that there are no mysterious conditions for, or methods of acquiring, such specialized knowledge and skills.

The problems of conducting research in the area of male homosexuality result, however, not only from the characteristic features of the homosexual world. They are also a function of the fact that the investigator's professional career and his professional rewards and support come from the larger society. Here the issue of the role problem for the male researcher in a male homosexual group is joined with that of the attributions of "special interests" or "motives" to the male professional who engages in research on male homosexuality. And again it may be said that, if the assumption that research on male homosexuality is taboo has validity, it is accounted for by this fact. The discouragement of male graduate students from entering the field because of the career hazards is well known. When I initiated the research project and was searching for sociological material, I was told by a prominent sociologist that there was none. He commented that no male researcher would dare enter the field because of the career hazards involved and added that I could do it because I was a woman. There is some encouraging evidence, however, that the situation is changing. Research reports in this field are being published by male investigators, and private communications with graduate students and with professional men more advanced in their careers indicate that the taboo is gradually being broken. Women researchers are not so likely to encounter such negative imputations from their colleagues, although curiosity about their selection of this particular research area is always lively.

With increasing amounts of data, it becomes possible to formulate theoretical problems of critical significance for all the behavioral sciences. As research on male homosexuality moves from its general and exploratory character to more precise formulation of issues, it is possible and, I think, highly probable that the effects of the imputations about the motives of the researcher for entering the field will diminish.

The investigator also encounters problems in relation to the community beyond his professional colleagues. One is the pressure exerted on the researcher to be a community consultant or agent of change while engaging in scientific research, the results of which are badly needed in order that such consultation may have a solid basis. Community organizations are constantly seeking advice on how to prevent and cure homosexuality. The pressure to help solve practical problems of management is considerable. It is difficult to cope with the demand for advice in these matters and to handle the delicate public-relations problems which arise. At the same time, pressure is being exerted on the researcher by homosexuals in an opposite direction—to plead their case for them to the community, to help change the laws, to help change social attitudes. Pressures for immediate solutions of these affect-laden issues add greatly to the stress of the research.

At the beginning of this paper, I was firm in stating a position that the problems involved in conducting scientific research on male homosexuality were not a function of a taboo on the inquiry itself. To document this position, I have described some of the problems which have arisen in the course of a long investigation, one which is still continuing. Although I have referred to issues which could arise for a male investigator, which, in the past, would have amounted to a taboo on the research itself, I have tried to show that the taboo is not universal even for male investigators. All the problems described could and do arise in scientific investigations of other areas of human behavior, although the specific content may be different. For example, all investigations of behavior which is subject to strong social or legal prohibitions involve special methods of finding research subjects if they are to be located in the community outside of institutions. All investigations of social groups the members of which tend to exclude outsiders require solutions to role problems of the observer in participant observation.

It is important not to lose the specific content of these problems in relation to the behavior under investigation. They are not merely "troubles" of the investigator which must be solved in order to get on with the scientific investigation. They constitute additional data to be used for the illumination of the phenomenon. In fact, for the theoretical formulation of the essential features of the homosexual world and the personality organization of its members, some of the most important data are the problems which we have described, of the difficulties of establishing trust, locating members, and managing a viable research role with respect both to the homosexual world and to the larger community.

Although the focus of this discussion has been on the difficulties of conducting scientific inquiry into male homosexuality in our society and the perspective within which they may be appropriately evaluated, I want to comment on the value of the inquiry and the highly gratifying rewards to the research investigator.

The implications of research findings for solutions to the complex personal and social issues associated with homosexuality are, of course, of large magnitude. Urgent pleas for empirical knowledge with which to formulate wise public policy are made by reflective and responsible persons in many walks of public as well as private life. The potential value of the research for human welfare is therefore incalculable. Critical decisions which may make all the difference between the complete waste of human potential and its constructive use may depend on it. To degrade or to dignify; to create despair or hope; to treat or to punish— the alternatives are too often sharply drawn. The researcher finds deep, enduring satisfaction in a contribution to such a fateful discussion.

For many investigators, the primary value of the research and the satisfactions resulting therefrom are to be found in its potential contribution to the solution of fundamental questions about the nature of man and society. The "challenge to science" (Silver, 1957) presented by homosexuality in understanding the basic social and biological processes which determine the patterns of sexual behavior in man, their correlates and consequences, is a formidable one. To respond to that challenge and to make even a small contribution to the solution of such a fundamental question is to find the kind of satisfaction which has always rewarded intellectual search and discovery.

■ Selected Bibliography ■

Bieber, I., Dain, H.J., Dince, P.R., Drellich, M.G., Grand, H.G., Gundlach, R.H., Kremer, Malvina W., Rifkin, A.H., Wilbur, Cornelia B., & Bieber, T.B. *Homosexuality*. New York: Basic Books, 1962.

Cory, D.W. *The homosexual in America: A subjective approach.* New York: Greenberg, 1951.

Curran, D., & Parr, D. Homosexuality: An analysis of 100 male cases seen in private practice. *Brit. med. J.*, 1957, 1, 787–801.

Davids, A., Joelson, M., & McArthur, C. Rorschach and TAT indices of homosexuality in overt homosexuals, neurotics and normal males. *J. abnorm. soc. Psychol.*, 1956, 53, 161–172.

Doidge, W.T., & Holtzman, W.H. Implications of homosexuality among Air Force trainees. *J. consult. Psychol.*, 1960, 24, 9–14.

Ford, C.S., & Beach, F.A. *Patterns of sexual behavior*. New York: Harpers, 1951.

Hooker, Evelyn. The adjustment of the male overt homosexual. *J. proj. Tech.*, 1957, 21, 1–31.

Hooker, Evelyn. Male homosexuality in the Rorschach. *J. proj. Tech.*, 1958, 22, 33–54.

Hooker, Evelyn. The homosexual community. In *Proceedings of the XIVth International Congress of Applied Psychology*. Copenhagen: Munksgaard, 1961. Pp. 40–59.

Kinsey, A.C., Pomeroy, W.B., & Martin, C.E. *Sexual behavior in the human male*. Philadelphia: W.B. Saunders, 1948.

Leznoff, M. Interviewing homosexuals. *Amer. J. Sociol.*, 1956, 62, 202–204.

Leznoff, M., & Westley, W.A. The homosexual community. *Social Probl.*, 1956, 3, 257–263.

Reiss, A.J., Jr. The social integration of queers and peers. *Social Probl.*, 1961, 9, 102–120.

Silver, G.A. The homosexual: A challenge to science. *The Nation*, May 25, 1957, 184, 451–454.

Thompson, Clara. Changing concepts of homosexuality. In P. Mullahy (Ed.), *A study of interpersonal relations*. New York: Grove Press, 1949.

Westwood, G. *A minority: A report on the life of the male homosexual in Great Britain*. London: Longmans & Green, 1960.

The Wolfenden report: Report of the Committee on Homosexual Offenses and Prostitution. New York: Stein & Day, 1963.

▪ 6 ▪

Parapsychology

Gardner Murphy

When Sir William Barrett, at a meeting of the British Association for the Advancement of Science, presented some new experimental findings in telepathy to the great Helmholtz, he got the ultimate scientific answer. The phenomena obviously could not have occurred. When Sir William said, "But I saw some of these phenomena myself," the reply, according to Barrett's record of the conversation was: "Neither the testimony of all the members of the British Association for the Advancement of Science, nor my own testimony from what my own eyes recorded, would convince me of telepathy, since it is manifestly impossible." This statement emphasizes the difference between the taboos in the areas of sex, death, and suicide and those with which I have to deal. Whereas my colleagues who work in the above areas are all guilty by association, that is, are concerned with things with which decent people do not deal, I am concerned with things that do not even exist.

As a matter of fact, I have had the pertinacity to persist for more than forty years in examining these phenomena, during which time the phenomena have increasingly proved to be out of touch with all basic, decent, scientific modes of thought. The issue, then, seems to be essentially whether the thought patterns which have developed in the past one hundred and fifty years regarding what the human mind is and can do must be strait-jacketed forever and forced to go on doing and being what we "know" the mind is and can do.

We are dealing essentially with the problem of respectability, and especially with the problem of scientific respectability. There is nothing more precious to most of us, in terms of self-image and professional goals, than to represent those sturdy, clear-eyed, honest men and women who have seen the great message of science. They have given up all their naïve, childish beliefs, all the things that plainly cannot exist within this strange, warm, impersonal universe, so full of intensely personal values which, nevertheless, must be put aside in the name of science. Among these are phenomena of apparitions or ghosts and phenomena which are metaphysically terrifying, like contact with distant objects by means other than the senses. Perhaps the ultimate and most terrifying phenomenon is contact with events which have not yet occurred, a phenomenon of precognition which, we will agree, is fundamentally antirational in terms of any scientific frame of reference which we take for granted. There is, therefore, a good deal more expected of young psychologists than willingness to accept a certain amount of derisive comment. There is a deeper question as to the personal adequacy of one who wants to give his life to something patently so disparate from the accepted images of science and of the scientific hero, that is, the man or woman willing to give his or her life for science, when the life is plainly too precious to be pawned out of mere curiosity.

The taboo in this field lies rather with the definition of what it is that is normally and properly scientific. There has been a great change—tactically, not strategically—in the past twenty or thirty years in regard to research in this field. When I talk to groups on parapsychology or if I am asked to give a talk on perception, I usually make sure that it is proper for me to introduce a few paragraphs on extrasensory perception. If I am asked to talk about the sociology of knowledge and its *Zeitgeist,* how we see things in terms of the time-space culture in which we are born and grow up, and I ask whether it will be all right to give illustrations in parapsychology, the answer is always enthusiastically affirmative. One no longer gets the heckling, the snide questions, of twenty or thirty years ago. This I must honestly grant: there has been a big change; one is welcome. But there is also a curious backward movement, reminding one of Newton's Third Law: for every action there is an equal and opposite reaction. Somehow, you push this boulder magnificently, and it does not budge. It is heroic to have the people gather around you and help to push, but still it does not budge. People do not laugh anymore, as they laughed at poor Sisyphus trying to make things budge in a permanent way. One would talk to audiences of earnest, devoted people who would like to know what someone odd enough to concern himself with this field is like and what data he believes actually available. They will be interested, but they will not read and check on this interesting matter. Even today, I wonder whether my words are having any more effect than when I talked on this topic four or five or fifteen years ago.

I think that there may be undercurrents of change. Lucien Warner has put us in his debt by three times surveying the data (two are available in detail) on the opinions of both old and young psychologists on the possibilities of work within this taboo area. We have slowly begun to show a certain willingness to give the other fellow the benefit of the doubt, but the old basic laws of respectability still rather clearly define what the nature of the mind is, what it can and what it cannot do. Areas which are taboo do not change rapidly, even under considerable corrosive influence. One is reminded here of what Conant so beautifully pointed out about the phlogiston theory, which, as you may remember, served for many years as an organizing principle in chemistry. About seventy-five years after the phlogiston theory was completely exploded—and was still being taught, of course, in standard fashion in the universities—the oxygen theory, credited to Priestley and his contemporaries, was finally so stated that it could conveniently take over all the phlogiston theories, ancillary findings as well as the theoretical structure. The important thing, Conant very rightly pointed out, is that we wait until a new theory is available before the old theory is dislodged. Any number of facts, said Conant, can be available, facts which will be solidly, brilliantly established by men in various laboratories, but these will not come into the structure of science until a theoretical system has developed which will be adequate to handle all the old facts and will displace the old system. I think that this conception of Conant and Mannheim's conception of the sociology of knowledge help us to realize that there is no point in deriding or attacking colleagues who regard our entire line of investigation as nonsensical and puerile, because their reactions are overdetermined in a complex way in terms of the structural system of cultural evolution and of scientific evolution in particular.

Look at the terms applied to parapsychology—"occultism," "mysticism," "the supernormal," "the paranormal," and "the psychic." These are, apparently, the five standard terms, and at least three of them have an unsavory flavor, which means that one would obviously be crazy to believe in them. Why should one accept a vocabulary which arbitrarily gives a predetermined position to a system of views? It is a tremendous problem to coin terms without the bathroom associations of the discredited, unpleasant terminology which has persisted within this sphere. Actually, since J.B. Rhine's book on extrasensory perception in 1934 broke open doors which previously had been closed and allowed the establishment of a university laboratory research unit on a larger scale, the problem has been one of getting young psychologists to orient themselves to the possibility that something beyond the taboo doors might actually exist. In fact, it has often been suggested in scientific as well as in political realms that the only way to get a change is to wait twenty or thirty years until the older people have moved on and people who have received different kinds of training have arrived on the scene. This would be essentially true, but there is the fact that the young people have to make a living, have to pursue power and prestige, and have to find a decent place for themselves in the halls of science. There has not been, in a world dominated by the psychological creeds of recent decades, any chance for the young person to get a stable academic position if he were interested in this line of research. Although it is not exactly disreputable to have some knowledge of research in such fields as telepathy, clairvoyance, and precognition, it is nevertheless practically impossible to make this a focus of one's research. I deal every year with many men and women who are searching for some sort of opportunity to do research in these fields. There are, to the best of my knowledge, about forty paid positions in this field in the world, and not a single one of them, so far as I know, is a permanently endowed, open position in which a person has the freedom to search over a long period for whatever nature presents without the serious likelihood that the discovery of material which is taboo would dislodge him professionally.

One might say that the change of tempo within the last few decades from a "slam-the-door" to a "let's-see" or "sit-tight" attitude is fine for the older people in psychology. I enjoy being able to talk about this topic and not getting heckled to death. When I lecture in a state hospital or in a university and I present the evidence the way I see it, citing experiment after experiment, I am asked good, realistic questions. I enjoy this give-and-take at a high level, something I had rarely been able to achieve before World War II. But this does not help me at all with the problem of young people who would like to go to work in this taboo field. Our problem is not whether people think we are intellectually respectable. We grant that we are not. Rather, we want to know whether we can start and maintain an experimental movement which will command interest and give an opportunity to eager, bright young people who might say: "Here is an opportunity to study the expansion of psychology into a vast realm in which it has been taboo. Here is the possibility of discovering a great many very fundamental things about human personality, all reaching out into all sorts of transpersonal realities just as exciting as the man-in-space program. Here is a possibility to see the limits, or limitlessness, of human personality in regard to time, space, and matter." It is an electrifying possibility. If we could get one young psychologist with ability and experience to commit himself or herself to this, then, even though several thousand people laughed to scorn, we would call it a very good bargain.

Actually, we older people are not in the kind of danger that some of our contemporaries were in the era of William James, when they were simply howled down. At least there has been this change. But the more fundamental issue, the thing that keeps the younger people from reading about, knowing about, coming into contact with, and beginning to make a research career for themselves in this area—this problem has not been solved.

I want to suggest at least six things which I think both parapsychologists and those working with them can do realistically. Some of these are rational, some are irrational, whereas others are typical of human nature, that is, a combination of the two.

First, experimental studies must be emphasized. The question of what really happened when a man saw an apparition, for example, of his wife's tragic death three thousand miles away, under conditions in which there is testimony at both ends of the circuit so that we know he saw the detailed nature of her death within a minute or two of this event—these are important facts in nature, but they are not *strategically* the kinds of event which will make a dent in the development of the science. On the other hand, experimental studies, even of a very limited type, of telepathic interaction would be able to make such a dent.

Second, the experiments should be done in ways that psychologists understand. If a better method exists, if various types of control are available which are even more severe than those ordinarily employed by psychologists, it is probably better not to use them. The controls, the methods, the statistics which are standard in the psychology of the period should be used. The attempt to employ double and triple safeguards in this field has usually just bored, confused, and frightened psychologists away from reading these studies. One must deal with human beings as they are and give them what they are demanding.

Third, there is today a good deal of prestige in research into all sorts of special states of mind and body—drug research, isolation research, hypnosis, studies of so-called altered states of consciousness, and many others. Many people believe that these states are highly conducive to telepathic and other paranormal phenomena. Perhaps they are, but whether they are or not it is important to work with the psychologist so that he knows that he is being worked with, not against; that there is a willingness to use the same drugs, the same hypnotic schedules; and that there is the same interest in a study of marginal awareness—all of which are the current thought patterns. If others are to understand, the work must be performed within the thought patterns which have become precious to them.

Fourth, the parameters, such as motivation and perceptual thresholds, used in any study of normal behavior must be emphasized. A fair amount of the study of subthreshold sensory perception leads to the possibility of including studies of extrasensory perception. Experiments must be devised to see how far extrasensory phenomena obey the same basic laws as ordinary sensory perception. Where there is quantitatively good work, this is an area which psychologists are likely to understand.

Fifth, one should work with other groups. There are always biologists, physicists, chemists, and mathematicians in universities who are interested in the problem, however reluctant the psychologists may be. In the university library, where the dusty old journals are tied up and the articles have not been looked at by anybody in the university for many years, may be found, in journals of cognate sciences, the evidence that no such severe prejudices exist. Many books by well-known neurologists, physicists, botanists, and so on which deal with extrasensory phenomena may be found. It is good to be in touch with the scientific spirit of today, and not only with the spirit of scientific psychology in its narrow sense. With work on an interdisciplinary or collaborative basis, the taboo will gradually erode as we find ourselves members of the scientific community.

Finally, it seems to me this has to be done along with all those other people who are asking similar questions in many other areas as to the nature of science itself. The people who are asking questions beyond operationalism or logical positivism are asking the most profound questions about the limits of knowledge and particularly of knowledge of human personality. If, over and over again, ever-patiently, experiments can be carried out which aim always at the ultimate standard of replicability, experiments which can be repeated by any competent laboratory person anywhere, this very spirit will define that broad scientific group consisting partly of scientists and partly of those others trying to explore in an ever-new way the horizons of a science of human nature which does not yet exist.

▪ Selected Bibliography ▪

Murphy, G. *The challenge of psychical research.* New York: Harper Bros., 1961.

Murphy, G., & Ballou, R.O. (Eds.) *William James on psychical research.* New York: Viking, 1960.

Myers, F.W.H. *Human personality and its survival of bodily death.* New York: Longmans, 1903. 2 vols.

Rhine, J.B., & Pratt, J.G. *Parapsychology: Frontier science of the mind.* Springfield: Charles C Thomas, 1957.

Woodruff, J.L. Some basic problems for parapsychological research. *J. Parapsychology,* 1948, 12, 123–125.

∎ 7 ∎

Graphology

Daniel S. Anthony

The basic factor which prevents the scientific investigation of graphology in America today is the paucity of psychologists who know enough about handwriting analysis to participate effectively in its investigation. Although this poverty of psychologically trained graphologists is presently being corrected, the long-range prospect of ameliorating the scarcity does not afford America's few practicing professional graphologists much cause for optimism.

In view of the complexity of the question and despite my cavalier assumption of one causal factor as the bedrock of the investigative problem, I should like to examine several other difficulties confronting graphology in our country today. Or, more to the point, why do so few graduate clinical psychologists know so little about handwriting analysis? What materials are currently available which could begin to satisfy the intellectual curiosity of the potential investigator of graphology's assets and liabilities as a psychodiagnostic device?

The answer to the first question is, I believe, palpably simple. So few know so little about the subject because there is only one college in America where it is taught. That institution, the New School for Social Research, in New York City, has offered two undergraduate elementary courses in graphology for more than fifteen years. No courses in graphology are yet available in its graduate school. Although the New School administration is maintaining a conservative attitude on graduate level accreditation for the subject, it is still, after fifteen years, the only college in the United States where an aspiring psychologist can get two credits for each of two graphology courses taken toward his bachelor's degree.

The answer to the second question—what materials are available for the serious student of handwriting analysis?—is somewhat more hopeful. There are many research materials, but none in textbook form, and few of them satisfy both graphologists and psychologists. Nevertheless, before the academic taboo against graphology can be fairly evaluated, one should have a better understanding of how and why academic antipathy to this questionable science has caused the intellectual aridity if not the experimental erosion on graphology's American frontier.

Certainly, both graphologists and psychologists have justifiable complaints. These conflicting attitudes and values begin, I believe, with the psychologists' lack of knowledge of the historical research in graphology on the continent of Europe. It has been stymied by the graphologists' inability to translate the language of handwriting analysis into the sophisticated concepts of modern experimental psychology. A brief exposition of the history may show that not all graphologists are intuitivists and aid in the search for the new paths to communication and research with the psychologists, who are needed for critical research and testing.

Webster's New Twentieth Century Dictionary (unabridged, 1958) defines graphology: "the study of handwriting, especially as it is *supposed*[1] to indicate the writer's character, aptitude, etc." The literature on graphology abounds with diverse and conflicting claims as to its utility, versatility, immutability, and reliability. Most psychologists limit the range of its current effectiveness, whereas almost all graphologists expand its predictability potential far beyond the confines of the highest correlations ever achieved. As in most other disciplines, the extremists can prove that they are right. But, from its use in medical and psychiatric diagnosis (Flückiger, Tripp, & Weinberg, 1961) through its growing application in business and industry (Anthony, 1960), much research has been attempted and some surprising results have been achieved.

At present, the case for graphology lies somewhere between complete acceptance and total rejection. It is my belief that future psychographologists will find graphology productive of a personality synthesis not yet achieved by other projective or expressive methods. Its present limitations are far more an indication of the graphologists' shortcomings than a measure of graphology's real but untapped potential.

The *Encyclopaedia Britannica* Library Research Service in 1959 issued a rather unusual amalgam of quotations from various authors as a ten-page monograph, "Graphology," a report which runs the gamut from sense to nonsense concerning "graphology, a stepsister of American psychology for so many years . . ." (Bell, 1948). The *Britannica* monograph, after four pages of Bell's good sense on handwriting analysis, digresses to the hodgepodge of nonsense reminiscent of the nineteenth-century single-trait graphology which gives many twentieth-century psychologists the perfect right to accept Webster's captious definition of *"supposed* to indicate . . . character." A reference to one of the monograph's many brash graphological hypotheses may explain this point more clearly. *"Short end strokes:*—Often part of a combination of factors showing malevolence or stubbornness."

Statements such as these are the mid-twentieth–century remnants of an earlier atomistic approach to the psychological inter-

[1] My italics.

pretation of graphic indicators. They are representative of a school of graphologic thought originally formulated in the seventeenth century in Italy by the physician Camillo Baldo (1664) and refined by the Abbé Jean-Hippolyte Michon (1872; 1875) in Paris. Known later as the "school of fixed trait signs," it called for a rather rigid, one-to-one, single-trait interpretation of such graphic phenomena as the "short end stroke" alluded to above. Michon coined the term "graphology," and from the ranks of his students grew the Société Graphologique, which continued in France until World War II. The obvious limitations of this atomistic approach became apparent to one of Michon's French successors, J. Crepieux-Jamin (1924; 1947), who shifted his emphasis from the single elements and letter forms, such as t-bars and i-dots, to the over-all, or global, configurations of the written page. He said: "The study of elements is to graphology as the study of the alphabet is to the reading of prose."

By the beginning of the twentieth century, the Continent's graphology focus transferred from France to Germany, where the brilliant young philosopher, Ludwig Klages (1923; 1936), became the German proponent of the exploratory "science" of handwriting analysis. He established the principles of contraction-balance-release and the expressive-movement theories which were to become the keystones of the experimentation and research which has placed German graphology in its pre-eminent position.

While European philosophers, physicians, psychiatrists, and psychologists were pursuing the study of graphology with some major breakthroughs, in America only June Downey (1919) at the University of Iowa showed any academic proficiency and interest in the subject until the arrival on the scene of Gordon W. Allport and Philip E. Vernon, who were preparing their *Studies in Expressive Movement* (1933) at the Harvard Psychological Clinic. These psychologists included handwriting in their investigations of human behavior on the assumptions that (1) personality is consistent, (2) movement is expressive of personality, and (3) the gestures and other expressive movements of an individual are consistent with one another.

Although their elaborate and painstaking experimentation

was not intended to validate the claims of professional graphologists, it showed the consistency of many forms of expressive activity, including handwriting, and exposed the "meaningful interrelation as well." Thus, the foundation for future research in graphology was well established by two sensitive and disciplined researchers at one of America's greatest seats of learning. The fact that few clinically trained researchers have taken advantage of Allport and Vernon's suggested designs for graphological research is one of many such questions awaiting plausible answer.

While Allport and Vernon were experimenting with graphology at Harvard, Thea Stein Lewinson came from Germany, where she had been studying the Klages method. In 1942, she and Joseph Zubin, an experimentally oriented psychologist, published their book, *Handwriting Analysis* (1942). It represented the first effort by either Europeans or Americans to devise a system for measuring and evaluating graphic indicators which would be amenable to rigorous research control and experimentation. The book is an explanation of the manner in which twenty-two graphic indicators can be quantified and qualified in accordance with psychologically acceptable standards of interpretation. The "Lewinson-Zubin Scale" resulting from this prodigious effort has been used by Lewinson and others on numerous studies.

The next major treatise to expose handwriting analysis to America's psychologists was included in John E. Bell's *Projective Techniques* (1948). His chapter on the development of modern graphology includes a bibliography of 137 references to graphological literature and experimental research and mentions most of the modern graphological exploration conducted up to 1948. The chapter includes an excellent section on scientific graphologic method based on the theories of Ludwig Klages, which could be considered a primer for curious psychologists.

Rose Wolfson (1949), writing in Anderson and Anderson (1951), impartially and objectively summarizes mid-twentieth–century graphological knowledge and includes an excellent capsule of the technique of the Lewinson-Zubin scales of contraction and release. She reports her own research on the usefulness of the Lewinson-Zubin approach to handwriting as a device for studying personality in delinquents. She concluded that the importance of the study was not in the statistical findings as such, but in the conclusions to be drawn regarding the scales themselves. She considered the scales a promising "anatomy," or geography, for handwriting which could guide the graphologically uninformed and serve investigators of handwriting as a common starting point. Most important, perhaps, the Lewinson-Zubin scales, in their combined atomistic and global structure and their objective treatment of "rhythm," offered a scientific means of investigating how sound judgments are made and the ways in which they can be extended.

Klara G. Roman's book, *Handwriting—A Key to Personality* (1952), is one of the few on graphology written in the English language which stems from a life of empirical research and experimentation. Although her research design and statistics may not meet all the rigorous standards of American experimentalists, her book is a brief but picturesque exposure of the most cultivated psychologist who practiced graphology in the Western world. Dr. Roman died as one of the few persons in the world capable of diagnosing speech disorders from samples of handwriting. She also worked in the early detection of emotional disturbances and predelinquent manifestations in the handwriting of children (1963).

Perhaps the most hopeful development in tearing down the roadblock to graphological investigation has been a fifteen-week workshop, "Graphology: A Psychodiagnostic Technique," conducted in 1963 for members of the Society for Projective Techniques in New York City. The New York chapter of the society was awarded a grant to support this workshop by the Human Ecology Fund, which sponsors research into environmental effects on human behavior. Rose Wolfson conducted the course, which emphasized the contraction and release movements in handwriting as they reflect correlates of personality.

In this connection, Gordon W. Allport has given me the opportunity to lecture before his graduate and undergraduate classes in personality and social psychology. He says: "My hope is that we can excite a few of these students to undertake future research of merit in the field."

In another direction, the Handwriting Institute, Inc., sponsored by Huntington Hartford, has perfected an electronic graphodyne for critical studies on speed and pressure of human writing. The effects of alcohol and of drugs on the motor behavior of ill and healthy subjects and other studies on the relations among various atomistic graphological letter-form variants and their relations to personality have been studied. The Handwriting Institute has attempted to test virtually the whole body of formal graphology against the known criterion variables of the Cattell clusters by use of machine computers.

In addition, the Handwriting Institute, in cooperation with various medical institutions and life insurance companies, has attempted to check the validity of Alfred Kanfer's Neuromuscular Test for Malignancy. Kanfer and Casten (1958) concerned themselves with purely physiological signs in handwriting, leaving aside possible psychological components. They used microscopic observations of writing strokes to investigate the neuromuscular coordination of cancer patients and classified typical aberrations of stroke quality, from which they predicted the presence or absence of cancer. The results were not only statistically significant, but sufficiently strong to support diagnostic prediction. Since early 1958, Alfred Kanfer has been a research associate at the Handwriting Institute, and his technique for interpreting various health factors in subjects according to microscopic neuromuscular irregularities that appear within ink strokes has been the subject of careful statistical and experimental examination. Certainly no other organization has ever matched the Handwriting Institute's high budget and intensive, high-level work on the unsolved reliability and validity problems that abound in graphology and the whole field of graphomotor expression.

Problems in the scientific investigation of handwriting analysis in America have grown out of a combination of historical, educational, and emotional factors. I believe that many of these difficulties can be attributed to the ready accessibility of handwriting and its too-easy availability for interpretation by unprofessional graphologists. Since the "Ideographia" of the Italian physician Camillo Baldo in the middle 1600's, the disorganized exploitation of handwriting analysis has been a plague on the healthy body of handwriting information as well as on its legitimate proponents.

Itinerant magicians of the seventeenth and eighteenth centuries laid the foundation for the addition of the fascinating revelations of handwriting to the repertoire of writers, artists, and intellectuals of the nineteenth century. But, while the medicine of bloodletting and the psychology of the humors gave way to the scientific advances of the Victorian era, graphology remained an easy prey to the untutored mystics of the nineteenth century.

Today in America, with the alarming success of a commercial enterprise which sells correspondence courses on handwriting analysis, more than ten thousand persons have been "trained" in the mysterious methods of revelation through the "hand." Most of these grammar school graduate "psychodiagnosticians" have never had a basic course in psychology. When they complete their twenty-five–cent analysis of a dupe's signature, the client may suspect the accuracy of the prognostication, but who is to say that it is not as good as a tealeaf reading which often costs a dollar? With these characters abounding on the boardwalks, in the cocktail lounges and parks of our nation, it is small wonder that most of the American public takes a dim view of handwriting analysis.

This brief excursion into the never-never land of the easy availability of fraudulent graphological knowledge explains in part, I believe, why handwriting analysis has been largely a taboo area for psychological investigation in the curriculums of American universities. Although this is only one of the many reasons for the university's rejection of handwriting analysis, it may well be that the other factors which contribute to the educators' doubts about graphology all radiate from this base. But German graphology seems to have originated from this same central point and terminated in a quite dissimilar academic environment. Why? Why did not Germany, the seat of modern psychology, contribute a more acceptable graphology to our national psychology along with its legacies of *Gestalt*, psychoanalytic, and projective psychology?

One of the important differences between the development of handwriting analysis in Germany and that in the United States has been the lack of trained, respected, acceptable professors and proponents of the difficult technique. Italy had its Baldo; France its Binet and Crepieux-Jamin; Germany its Kraepelin, Meyer, Preyer, Klages, and Pophal; and Switzerland its Pulver—all of whom spent good parts of their academic careers seeking empirical and experimental validation of graphological hypotheses. In addition to being men of knowledge and distinction, they were university-centered researchers of the growing art of graphological interpretation.

America has had no such psychologically trained disciples of handwriting analysis. June Downey (1919); Allport and Vernon (1933); Pascal (1943a; 1943b); Castelnuovo-Tedesco (1948); Cantril, Rand, and Allport (1933); Booth (1937; 1939); Secord (1949); Goodenough (1945); and all the other university psychologists who have conducted research on graphology make no claim, so far as I know, to graphological proficiency. They are psychologists devoted to their individual research, which at one time included handwriting analysis.

In Germany, no current student of graphology at the graduate level can be licensed to practice graphology after graduation without having first passed a minimum of six semester courses in the subject.[2] After the academic work is satisfactorily concluded, the future graphologist must pass a state licensing examination administered by one of the university-centered departments of psychology.

At least six West German universities include graphology in the clinical or applied psychology curriculum. I have been told that there are now approximately five hundred licensed graphologists in West Germany. Many of the superior students have chosen to continue their researches and are beginning to

[2] Pre-World War II graphologists without academic degrees were admitted to practice on the basis of experience and examination only.

do original work in uncharted areas. It is these graphologists who are accomplishing some of the controlled research on the many trait variables of handwriting which have previously proved so difficult to quantify and correlate (Wintermantel, 1957).

So far, we have been discussing the general problems of a deeper and more meaningful investigation of graphology. Let us now consider a few problems literally indigenous to handwriting itself.

First, of course, is the fact that almost everyone in America does write; therefore, everyone, whether he agrees to it or not, may be subject to an unsolicited graphological analysis. The threat of this illicit use of the graphologist's art is, I believe, often a negative conditioner. It has helped to make graphology suspect, if not taboo.

There is also the old complaint that, since we are all taught to write a certain way, graphology is invalid because handwriting is a learned method or a copied behavior pattern which we maintain throughout our lives. This patently absurd argument hardly requires refutation, but it is interesting to recall that some of the early investigators of graphology in this country utilized this specious, a priori assumption against handwriting analysis.

Far more realistic is the complaint that the easy accessibility of specimens for "diagnosis" makes handwriting analysis a damaging projective technique, because any person able to read a thirty-five–cent paperback book on the subject can become a self-ordained handwriting expert. I am afraid that the professional graphologist has no ready answer to this complaint. It is a valid one and in many ways the strongest polemic against graphology. It is the sincere hope of every professional graphologist that an eventual licensing system will prevent these self-appointed analysts from plying their trade in the psychological marketplace, but that halcyon day has not yet dawned.

Probably the most knotty enigma blocking the cooperation of graphologists and experimentalists in fundamentally sound research is the difficulty of quantifying the all-too-numerous and "imponderable" graphic variables. This complexity is further exacerbated by the fact that modern global graphologists refuse to be shackled to the single-trait, fixed-sign, atomistic method of psychological interpretation; therefore, *how* to validate *what* becomes a real question to be answered, lest the ghosts of Hull and Montgomery (1919) continue to haunt us.

I believe that it can be answered only when psychologists and graphologists have learned to speak the same language and can sit down together to plan their research designs. The Handwriting Institute, which has now had eight years of experience in this field, is a logical source of consultation. To my knowledge, there is no satisfactory way in which an experimental psychologist can evaluate graphic indicators unless he is also an experienced graphologist, able to cope with the qualitative variables which abound in the theory of handwriting analysis, just as they do in the expressive human behavior from which graphological theory derives.

It begins to look as though graphology is so complicated by its plethora of qualitative variables that any but the trained researcher-psychologist-graphologist is subject to immobilizing discouragement at the very inception of his research. This is another serious roadblock to investigation and objective experimentation. It is not, however, an insoluble problem once the universities begin to offer courses in graphology to those clinicians who would like to do research or utilize its diagnostic advantages in their psychotherapy practices.

Another hurdle on the road to graphological investigation in this country is the lack of textbooks from which the independent student or university scholar can get an appreciation of experimental handwriting methodology. To be sure, Allport and Vernon (1933); Lewinson and Zubin (1942); Wolfson (1949); Bell (1948); Roman (1952); Tripp, Flückiger, and Weinberg (1959); and Flückiger, Tripp, and Weinberg (1961) suggest many investigatory techniques in their specialized studies. However, few actually explain the research designs in textbook detail. Beginning students in a previously stigmatized area of research certainly should be given the luxury of an adequate textbook, but none is available in English. Thorny questions about graphology can never be removed until colleges train graphologists to turn out the research which can be reproduced in modern textbooks for succeeding college generations.

Future experimental researchers should have pointed out to them several advantages of handwriting analysis over many other projective devices in use today. For example, it can be used by the psychologist in the absence of the subject or tester. It affords a method for long-distance or *in absentia* interview and psychodiagnostic procedures. Graphology can be used as a supplementary psychodiagnostic tool whenever the patient or applicant has written extensively on other parts of the interviewing battery, such as the biographical information form or a sentence-completion response sheet. To be sure, these restricted specimens are not ideal for analysis, but, short of a few full pages of original, natural graphic construction, they can be advantageously used.

Handwriting analysis can also be helpful in two other important areas of psychological research—historical questions and management evaluation.

Most proud parents have kept samples of their children's handwriting and drawings since the first crayon scratches on the dining room wall. From the early struggles with print-script through the "at home" life of the socializing child, handwriting specimens, diaries, and letters frequently become a permanent record of individual growth and development. In a diagnostic or therapeutic situation, therapists can now have graphological analyses of the early stages in the psychosexual maturing process of their patients. There would be no reason, when graphology is an accepted procedure, why specimens of one's handwriting should not be utilized to understand the periods of psychic crisis or psychosocial advancement in an individual's adjustment.

Likewise, handwriting analysis should be of inestimable value in re-creating the psychosocial development of historical figures and famous people, deceased and living. Could it not be used to help shed light on the continuing riddle, for instance of Leonardo da Vinci's psychosexual ambivalence or Vincent van Gogh's reasons for suicide?

75

Specifically, far greater use could be made of the posthumous analysis of scripts of suicides and suicidal personalities, once psychologists start collaborating with trained graphologists.

In business, industry, and governmental organizations, much of the responsibility for failure or firing has been attributed to the employee. The employer was usually, if not always, right, simply because he was boss. Today, with the nascent psychological sensitivity of management and the power of labor unions, the old situation no longer prevails. Alert executives and personnel directors are aware of the selection, analysis, nurture, and development of supervisors, managers, and junior executives. It is indeed possible that such a readily available technique as handwriting analysis can be utilized to describe the important behavior characteristics of these executives before placing under them salesmen or subordinate personnel who may obviously (according to their graphological analysis) clash with that all-too-independent variable, the boss's personality.

To summarize, the present status of handwriting analysis in America appears to be the following:

Since no graduate clinical psychology curriculum in any American university offers the subject, we have insufficient trained psychographologists to conduct the necessary research which might begin to lend more respectability and reliability to handwriting analysis.

Because of this yawning void in training facilities and the consequent dearth of trained graphologists, there is no true clearinghouse or caretaker agency responsible for leadership and control of standards of licensing procedure.

Owing to these conditions and the lack of academic standards or controls, graphology's unique fascination has been parlayed by the shrewd clip artist looking for a panacea for his personal and financial frustrations. The "easy art" of handwriting analysis has answered the needs of the drawing room psychologizers who seek a dramatic new path to personal popularity.

Add to this overwhelmingly negative bill of particulars the fact that no American university has accepted the challenge of translating the expanding body of experimental research conducted over the past ten years in German universities, and the ethical future of graphology remains in question.

Although some individual professional graphologists practicing in this country today are familiar with the significant German research on handwriting analysis, few of these professionals have been given the chance to transmit the vital information to the next generation of psychologists now in training. A few universities appear ready to rectify this practice.

It is my personal feeling that much valuable time will be saved if the recent German research is digested in palatable American idiom. One or two of the better German textbooks might be translated into English. A knowledge of this work is, I think, one of the necessary precursors to future academic interest in graphology and the foundation for more scientific research which would take place in America thereafter.

Finally, whether we get German translations or not; whether universities do or do not regularize graphology in the graduate projective-psychology curriculums; and whether or not charlatans continue to flourish in the amusement parks of our nation, it is my conviction that we shall one day view graphology as an integral part of our psychodiagnostic batteries. For, just as psychoanalysis and the Rorschach protocol have broken the barriers of professional conservatism, so eventually will graphology earn its place as a unique method of assessing man's conscious and unconscious expressive behavior.

■ Selected Bibliography ■

Allport, G.W., & Vernon, P.E. *Studies in expressive movement.* New York: Macmillan Co., 1933.

Anderson, H.H., & Anderson, G.L. (Eds.) *An introduction to projective techniques.* Englewood Cliffs, N.J.: Prentice-Hall, Inc., 1951.

Anthony, D.S. *Digest of workshop.* San Jose, Calif.: American Handwriting Analysis Foundation, 1960.

Baldo, C. *Trattaro come da una lettera missiva si conoscono la natura e qualita del scrittore.* Bologna. 1664.

Bell, J.E. *Projective techniques.* New York: Longmans, Green & Co., 1948.

Booth, G.C. The use of graphology in medicine. *J. nerv. ment. Dis.*, 1937, **86**, 674–679.

Booth, G.C. Objective techniques in personality testing. *Arch. Neurol. Psychiat.*, 1939, **42**, 514–530.

Cantril, H., Rand, H.A., & Allport, G.W. The determination of personal interests by psychological and graphological methods. *Charact. & Pers.*, 1933, **2**, 134–143.

Castelnuovo-Tedesco, P. A study of the relationship between handwriting and personality variables. *Genet. Psychol. Monogr.*, 1948, **37**, 167–220.

Crepieux-Jamin, J. *Les éléments de l'écriture des canailles.* Paris: Presses Universitaires, 1924.

Crepieux-Jamin, J. *L'écriture et le caractère.* [1895] Paris: Presses Universitaires, 1947.

Downey, June E. *Graphology and the psychology of handwriting.* Baltimore: Warwick & York, 1919.

Flückiger, F.A., Tripp, C.A., & Weinberg, G.H. A review of experimental research in graphology, 1933–1960. *Percept. mot. Skills, Monogr. Suppl.*, 1961, **12**, 67–90.

Goodenough, Florence L. Sex differences in judging the sex of handwriting. *J. soc. Psychol.*, 1945, **22**, 61–68.

Hull, C.L., & Montgomery, Ruth P. Experimental investigation of certain alleged relations between character and handwriting. *Psychol. Rev.*, 1919, **26**, 63–74.

Kanfer, A., & Casten, D.F. Observations on disturbances in neuromuscular coordination in patients with malignant disease. *Bull. Hosp. Joint Dis.*, 1958, **19**, 1–19.

Klages, L. *Ausdrucksbewegung und gestaltungskraft.* Leipzig: J.A. Barth, 1923.

Klages, L. *Handschrift und charakter.* Leipzig: J.A. Barth, 1936.

Lewinson, Thea Stein, & Zubin, J. *Handwriting analysis.* New York: King's Crown Press, 1942; reprinted by University Microfilm Inc., Ann Arbor, Mich., 1963.

Michon, J.H. *Les mystères de l'écriture.* Paris: Presses Universitaires, 1872.

Michon, J.H. *Système de graphologie.* Paris: Presses Universitaires, 1875.

Pascal, G.R. The analysis of handwriting: A test of significance. *Charact. & Pers.,* 1943, **12**, 123–144.

Pascal, G.R. Handwriting pressure: Its measurement and significance. *Charact. & Pers.,* 1943, **12**, 235–254. (b)

Roman, Klara G. Handwriting and speech: A study of the diagnostic value of graphic indices for the exploration of speech disorders. *Logos,* 1959, **2**, 29–39.

Roman, Klara G. *Handwriting—a key to personality.* New York: Pantheon Books, Inc., 1952.

Roman, Klara G. Graphology. *Encyclop. ment. Hlth.* New York: Grolier, 1963. Pp. 679–702.

Secord, P.F. Studies of the relationship of handwriting to personality. *J. Pers.,* 1949, **17**, 430–448.

Tripp, C.A., Flückiger, F.A., & Weinberg, G.H. Effects of alcohol on the graphomotor performances of normals and chronic alcoholics. *Percept. mot. Skills,* 1959, **9**, 227–236.

Wintermantel, F. *Bibliographia graphologica.* Stuttgart: Ruhle-Diebener Verlag KG., 1957

Wolff, W. *Diagrams of the unconscious.* New York: Grune & Stratton, 1948.

Wolfson, Rose. *A study in handwriting analysis.* Ann Arbor, Mich.: Edwards Brothers, Inc., 1949.

Wolfson, Rose. Graphology. In H.H. Anderson & Gladys L. Anderson (Eds.), *An introduction to projective techniques.* Englewood Cliffs, N.J.: Prentice-Hall, Inc., 1951.

▪ 8 ▪

Religion

William Douglas

That religion should be a researchers' "taboo topic" in the mid-twentieth century would have surprised social scientists in the first quarter of the century. The psychology of religion seemed then off to a good beginning in the pioneer work of Hall, Starbuck, Coe, Pratt, and Leuba and was widely "advertised" in the 1901–1902 Gifford Lectures of William James on *The Varieties of Religious Experience* (1903). Great theoretical contributions were being made by Durkheim and Weber in sociology of religion and by Radcliffe-Brown and Malinowski in social anthropology. Studies by Tylor and Frazer of primitive religion and its symbolic artifacts stimulated much interest. Provocative theses had been advanced and conceptual models had been made available for further testing and refinement.

With such a promising beginning, why did the psychology of religion and, to a lesser extent, the sociology and anthropology of religion fail to develop in the second quarter-century as one might have expected? This question defies simple or definitive answer, but some of the contributing factors can be identified. More than fifty years ago, Pratt (1908) expressed an uneasiness which proved prophetic:

> Our book-shelves and our periodicals are laden with works on "religious psychology," most of which prove on examination to be hardly more psychological than anatomical or geographical. . . .
>
> Fondness for facts seems at times almost a blind craving. Meaning and perspective are often disregarded and forgotten in the worship of the naked fact. . . .
>
> Use of the questionnaire method has frequently been uncritical, and . . . physiological phraseology and fanciful explanations of complex states . . . seem often an attempt at too great simplification . . . [without having] fully learned the use of its tools. . . .
>
> We are in the midst of a serious religious crisis. . . . The old authorities and the old arguments for the religious view of the world are yearly, even daily, losing their hold over the community.

Pratt's comments were shown to be prophetic by later developments:

(1) "Religious psychology," still the preferred term in Europe, failed to differentiate itself from theology, philosophy of religion, and the general dogmatic and evangelistic task of the religious institution as a valid branch of general psychology.

(2) However, in the desperate effort to be recognized as "scientific," there was tremendous emphasis on the accumulation of discrete facts and their mathematical representation, without raising questions of theoretical or statistical significance or relating facts to one another in terms of general principles and comprehensive theory.

(3) Furthermore, the use of data-collection methods and explanatory concepts and theories was often uncritical and incompetent according to generally accepted scientific canons.

(4) The climate of public opinion was changing, at an in-

creasing rate after 1920, away from a religious and toward a naturalistic, behavioristic, and positivistic world view.

The psychology of religion failed to develop, then, because it still sought to serve the ends of the religious institution in the midst of a culture which was increasingly rejecting the authority of that institution and because it was seeking to be scientific without either adequate conceptualization of the problems to be investigated or rigorous methodology according to current scientific canon.

Similar factors appear to have operated (Honigsheim, 1957; Moberg, 1962) in the sociology and anthropology of religion.[1] In the effort to emulate physical science, there was a preoccupation with equilibrium models (for example, entropy) and system analysis. Older evolutionary theories were being attacked, as in the criticism of *The Golden Bough* (1959) and Malinowski's functional distinction between *Magic, Science, and Religion* (1925), but—as has been said of the contributions of Boas to anthropology—the introduction of scientific practices without sufficient undergirding theory left the social sciences confused and perplexed, but with the fragmentary rudiments of true science.

In addition to the four factors discussed above, two others appear to have operated: (1) the study of religion was inevitably conflictual for both researcher and subject because of the personal "investments" which might be challenged; and (2) the history of the development of social science as a whole opposed interest in this type of phenomena.

As long as one investigated primitive religion or distant cultures and historical periods, one could maintain reasonable "objectivity," without threat to personal or social commitments. As long as the object of study was adolescent emotional conversion, a socially deviant cult, or medieval mysticism and saintliness, one's own system of beliefs and practices could remain relatively unchallenged. But, as soon as study of "normal religious experi-

[1] Focus hereafter will be on American psychology and, in theology, on Protestant Christianity. Unfortunately, this provincialism has been typical of American scientific investigation of religion, in contrast to European scholarship.

ence" in one's own cultural setting and period began, difficulties were inevitable.

Indeed, this may be one reason why the sociology and anthropology of religion have become better established within their parent disciplines than has psychology of religion—the "in-here" aspect of psychological dynamics, in contrast to the relatively "out-there" quality of social systems and cultural processes. Social values may have a safer distance than personal values; institutional forms, even creeds and rituals, can probably be handled with less "numinous radiation" danger than can personal commitments and devotional life.

Subjective phenomena would, moreover, tend to be avoided by a developing social science which sought to be "empirical" and "objective." The anecdotal approach of early studies, with their relatively uncritical use of such source documents as travelers' reports (cf. *The Golden Bough*) or autobiographies (cf. James's *Varieties . . .*), was no longer acceptable. As psychology, in particular, tried to emulate its older brother, physics—"We have experimental method and laboratories, too"—it desperately sought to attain independence from its possessive mother, philosophy, and its dogmatic grandmother, theology. When others doubted its legitimacy as a true child of the sciences, it wondered itself to which branch of the family it belonged—natural, biological, or social.

But, as the social sciences were changing, moving from dependent infancy into rebellious adolescence, so was physics changing. While psychology sought to disassociate itself from philosophy, physics formed new alliances with it. While psychology sought "objectivity," post-Newtonian physics increasingly operated on the basis of a field theory which, as in Heisenberg's principle of indeterminacy, recognized that the observer was part of the observation event. (Cf. Jung's [1958, p. 592] principle of synchronicity, which he relates to "the ancient Chinese mind" expressed in the *I Ching*.)

Likewise, while most psychologists continued to accept a Cartesian subject-object dualism, which predicated that the categories of "reality" were isomorphic with those of conception and language, the natural sciences increasingly rejected the subject-object distinction. While psychologists sought "naked facts," such philosophers as Collingwood (1946) were demonstrating the inextricable intertwining of "fact" and "interpretation."

While psychologists in particular and social scientists in general worshipped methodology to the point that the form and language of communication became more important than the message (thus the truism that William James could not have had an article published in a modern psychological journal), data-collection and -analysis methods were in the midst of revolutionary developments. While the "grammar" of research technique and statistical method became the operational norms for social scientists, the theoretical basis of these norms, the conditions necessary for their application, were increasingly challenged.

It is small wonder, then, that religion should be a researchers' "taboo topic." For a generation reared on Freud's *The Future of an Illusion*, to have become interested in religion as a valid object of investigation would have been to be regarded as "tender-minded," "mystical," or "really a philosopher—not a psychologist at all." Such charges were, and to a lesser extent still are, applied not only to investigators of religion, but also to all others concerned with the "humanistic"—as distinguished from the strictly experimental and/or "valueless," descriptive—approach to social science. Therefore, in the period of about 1925 to 1950, serious attention to the religious quest as a valid aspect of human behavior was an interest not reinforced by professional sanctions.

But, if social science ceased to be interested in religion, did religion maintain an interest in social science? In general, the answer is, "no." Although the seminaries have seen successive "booms" in social ethics, religious education, and pastoral counseling, there has been relatively little interest or investment in the theoretical issues underlying and informing these applied subject matters. "Baptized and applied" social science could be fitted under a general heading of "practical theology," "pastoral theology," "social ethics," or "religious education," but the psychology and sociology of religion, as respectable theoretical dis-

ciplines, got no further off the ground in the theological seminaries than they did in the secular universities.

Indeed, in a theological seminary or church-related college,
the scientific investigation of religion was as apt to be a "taboo
topic" as among social scientists. Here, however, the problem
was not with "tender-minded" religion, to be given up for
"tough-minded" science as one became "educated for reality,"
but rather with "antireligious" science. As institutional religion
manned the ramparts in "the war between science and religion"
and particularly as it felt it was losing the war, the "godless
Freudian" psychologist or "economic-determinist-Marxian" sociologist was definitely not *persona grata.*

Since the end of World War II, however, the *Zeitgeist* has
been changing rapidly. There are many indications of a new
climate, among them the symposium from which this book grew.
When "taboo topics" are lifted to the respectability of an American Psychological Association annual convention, they are no
longer really "taboo." Likewise, when the president-elect of the
APA invites a professor of New Testament to speak on "The
Apostle Paul and the Introspective Conscience of the West," at
an annual convention and a large audience listens with respect,
if not overt enthusiasm, religion can no longer be really "taboo"
in these halls. Addresses on the psychology of religion have been
delivered at recent international congresses of psychology, and
colloquiums held at annual meetings of the American Psychological and Sociological associations.

Perhaps even more significant, the past decade has seen the
founding of new societies and journals dedicated to, among other
objectives, the scientific investigation of religion. Though the
Religious Education Association and the Society for the Scientific
Study of Religion had their origins prior to 1950, both groups
have made increasing contributions to knowledge in the past
decade, as has the Academy of Religion and Mental Health.
Though the academy's *Journal* has not, to date, focused on empirical research, two other new publications have—the semi-
annual *Journal for the Scientific Study of Religion* (1961 *et seq.*)

and the quarterly *Review of Religious Research* (1959 *et seq.*). The latter is published by the Religious Research Association, which continues a long and eminent tradition of social survey and research concerning the functioning of religious institutions.

Furthermore, the psychology and sociology of religion appear more firmly entrenched in both theological education and higher secular education than at any time in the past. Instruction in courses entitled "psychology of religion" goes back more than fifty years in Protestant theological education (Hartford, 1899—a course; Boston, 1912—a department). In a 1943 survey by Hiltner, almost two-thirds of the seminaries had at least one course in this field. But the influence of academic psychology on these courses seemed minimal; no professor held a full-time appointment in the field (as distinguished from pastoral care, counseling, religious education, pastoral theology, and so on), and only four had had graduate training in academic psychology.

Modest gain is shown over the past twenty years, with at least three full-time appointments in the psychology of religion in the academic year 1962–1963 and all incumbents holding membership in the American Psychological Association on the basis of earned doctorates. For higher secular education, an indication of change is the introduction of undergraduate instruction in the psychology of religion at Yale and Chicago. Also, judging from *Dissertation Abstracts,* there has been an increasing number of doctoral dissertations concerned with the scientific investigation of religion. And, judging by accepted criteria of social science research, their quality appears to be steadily rising.

Reference has already been made to the founding of new journals particularly concerned with the scientific investigation of religion. (Cf. the irregularly published *Journal of Religious Psychology and Education,* founded by G. Stanley Hall in 1904, and the monthly *Zeitschrift für Religionspsychologie,* founded by Johannes Bresler in Halle in 1907.) In addition, the past ten to twenty years have seen more and better articles concerned with religion in such journals as *The American Sociological Review, The American Journal of Sociology, Journal of Social Issues,* and *Social Forces,* though psychological journals, or, more probably, psychologists, have not kept pace. In terms of book publication, even excluding texts in the psychology and sociology of religion (Clark, 1958; Johnson, 1959; Moberg, 1962), a new interest by social scientists in religion is also manifest. For example, in one recent three-year period, these books appeared: Festinger, Riecken, and Schachter's *When Prophecy Fails* (1956), Sargant's *Battle for the Mind* (1957), Bakan's *Sigmund Freud and the Jewish Mystical Tradition* (1958), Erikson's *Young Man Luther* (1958), and Schneider and Dornbusch's *Popular Religion* (1958).

If the above indicators do represent valid and sufficient evidence of revived interest in religion as a field of investigation for social scientists and if religion is, therefore, becoming less a "taboo topic," how can one explain this phenomenon? Clearly, as with most issues of fundamental human concern, multiple causation operates. One can only guess (or, in professional terminology, formulate hypotheses) concerning contributory factors. Indeed, it is difficult even to establish dates for the beginning or apparent diminishing of the "taboo-topic" phase. In general terms, the 1900–1924 quarter-century might be designated as a promising infancy, the 1925–1949 quarter-century as a period of general stagnation and withdrawal, but with "stirrings" toward the end of the period, and the period following 1959 as one of renewed growth in the scientific investigation of religion. (An alternative, and perhaps more precise, formulation would be pre-1922, 1922–1943, and post-1944.)

What helped to produce this Toynbee-style advance-withdrawal-advance pattern, which also reminds one of Gesell's schema of child development? In part, it may (as with children) have been simply the passage of time. The deaths of James in 1910, Durkheim in 1917, and Weber in 1920, with posthumous publication of much of Weber's most important work in sociology of religion, marked in a sense the end of an era. Except perhaps for Malinowski (1884–1942), there was no one of their stature in social science ready and willing to continue their investigations of religion. Those who were to make later contributions, such as Gordon Allport, Talcott Parsons, and Clyde Kluckhohn (who participated in the founding of the interdisciplinary Department of Social Relations at Harvard in 1946), were not yet embarked on their professional careers. It took time after 1920 just to sift, digest, and comprehend the massive theoretical contributions of these pioneers. (In Weber's case, in particular, there was also a time lag between publication and translation into English.)

In addition, to use Weber's own conceptual framework as it has been developed by Parsons, an "instrumental-adaptive" mood, such as characterized the 1920's and 1930's, did not support the development of the scientific investigation of religion as would the "interest-teleological" (meaning) emphasis of post-World War II American society. In reaction against the earlier reformers, social scientists of the second quarter of the century usually sought to be as valueless and disinterested as possible, with a neat stimulus-response operationalism wherever possible. Facts, not meanings, were desired; "pure science" was the goal, not insightful understanding or change of personal or social conditions.

But, as Muelder (1951) states, such disinterestedness was hard to maintain, for:

> If the Great Depression with its predominantly economic and emergency governmental emphasis gave to the social scientist new roles and to social engineering a new significance, World War II made heavy demands on psychologists and anthropologists in addition because of the challenge of racism and the defense of democratic values and ideals. Scientists were called upon to commit themselves and their science. . . . The problem of universal norms could no longer be side-stepped in what many had tried to keep as value-free domains. Significant social problems drove the scientist beyond traditional positivism (p. 100).

Symbolic of this new approach and mood and acting as stimulus to further change was Myrdal's 1944 publication of *An American Dilemma*, which moved beyond social analysis to problems of conscience. Similarly, Kluckhohn's *Mirror for Man* (1949), Allport's *The Individual and His Religion* (1950), and Parson's *The*

Social System (1951) all emphasized the critical individual and social significance of questions of meaning and value.

Deep involvement in the war effort on the part of social scientists, especially in such agencies as the Office for War Information, stimulated their interest in problems of social psychology and anthropology and also led to the forced development of theory and method in a summer analogous to the wartime development of nuclear physics. In addition, clinical psychology received tremendous impetus through wartime needs for personality assessment, including the program of the Office for Strategic Services, directed by Henry A. Murray, and through postwar training programs of the Veterans Administration. Thus, the balance of the power structure in American psychology was tipped from the "rat-and-pigeon" experimentalists to the personality, social, and clinical psychologists, and there was much more support for such concerns as those expressed by the Society for the Psychological Study of Social Issues. With Murray (1963), I hope that the next step will be that of "integrating the endeavors of experimental specialists with those of personologists engaged in a multiform assessment program."

American social science and the culture of which it is a part, have, therefore, become much more willing to consider issues of meaning, value, and commitment as important and indeed inescapable. There is growing acceptance of Maslow's contention (1959) that "the ultimate disease of our time is valuelessness" (diagnosis) and, furthermore, that "something can be done about it by man's own rational efforts" (prognosis). To be concerned with issues of meaning and value does not, of course, necessarily mean study of religious commitment and practice. Yet, this has apparently been the necessary first step. "Values," vague as they are, have somehow seemed more objective and less personally threatening than "faith," "commitment," or "religion." Though there is much confusion in current social-scientific value theory and research (Tisdale, 1961), advances have been made. And, this has proved a "respectable" approach to the still partly taboo topic of religion.

A simple change in social and professional climate would

not, however, have been a sufficient condition of renewed scientific investigation of religion. *Quantitative* increase in the number of researchers and empirical studies had to be undergirded by *qualitative* improvement in research, dependent on the adequacy of training of the researcher, but, even more basically, on the theoretical and methodological tool kit available to him. It is, therefore, significant and hopeful for further advance that the developing format of the *Journal for the Scientific Study of Religion* should be tripartite: theoretical problems (including, on occasion, a symposium such as the one on "The Problem of Attempting to Define Religion" in the fall, 1962, issue), methodological problems, and empirical studies. It is also significant, in terms of American social scientists' general ignorance of non-contemporary and foreign investigations, that there should be a historical-bibliographical section (fall, 1961, devoted to Ernst Troeltsch) to supplement the standard reviews of current literature.

Development of research methods appropriate to the investigation of personal beliefs and the behaviors which express and reinforce them has been substantial in the past ten to twenty years. Until then, researchers were still employing the tools of the period of William James, particularly the questionnaire, and on the whole not so well as James, for there was general disregard of personal documents as source materials. Methods of investigation were crude and tended to miss the heart of the issues. Tallies of frequency of particular "beliefs" (that is, responses to questionnaire items); of such "religious practices" as prayer; and of affiliation with and support of the religious institution were, on the whole, not very illuminating. (Also, the majority of studies had college students, the captive population for university-based researchers, as subjects. There is much raw material here for future anthropological subculture studies!)

Manifest behavioral data, usually at least once removed, since they consisted of what the subject was able and willing to report, were taken as indicating latent variables which had some relation to "religion." But the exact nature of the indicator-concept relationship was never quite clear. And the things which the researcher could "get at" never seemed to be the really basic issues; the "nothing but" of the often-reductionist researcher was met by the "something more" of the often-defensive dogmatist.

Basic and perhaps fundamentally insoluble problems remain in terms of manifest-latent, indicator-concept relationships in the scientific investigation of religion. But it is a major advance that we are at least aware of the problems and the limitations which they impose on research findings and their interpretation.

Methodological advances have been promising, if not completely satisfying. They include:

1. improvement of the validity and reliability of both the questionnaire and interview as data-collection methods;

2. development of replicable and more than impressionist methods of content analysis of "unstructured" materials;

3. adaptation of such projective techniques as sentence completion, "draw a person," and the T.A.T. to areas "broader" than individual personality assessment and the beginning of development of reliable scoring and summary methods;

4. the Q-technique and recent adaptations, for example, Loomis's work with "doctrinal Q-sort";

5. semantic differential procedures and related approaches to the measurement of meaning and location of concepts in "semantic space";

6. a more holistic approach to belief and value analysis, as in Morris' "Ways of Life";

7. scaling techniques and clarification of their underlying theory, especially by Guttman;

8. statistical techniques more relevant to the data of the social sciences, such as nonparametric and factor-analytic

techniques, as well as increased specification of the adequacy and range of generalization of data in terms of measures of statistical significance and sampling theory; and

9. the possibility of large-N, precise-detail, multivariate data analysis by high-speed electronic computers.

Although these advances in methodology have revolutionized all of social science, they have been of particular assistance in investigating the complex phenomena involved in religious commitment, belief, and behavior. Still more significant and promising regarding future research have been recent theoretical advances. Inadequate conceptualization, especially of necessary distinctions and discriminations, has handicapped the scientific investigation of religion almost as much as a limited tool kit.

In recent decades, social scientists have become much more exact in defining the connotations and denotations of such terms as "religion" and have discovered, among other things, that James, Jung, and Freud were seeking to describe quite different phenomena when they used roughly parallel terminology. Awareness has also increased of how the researcher's personal philosophy and value system shape his selection of subjects for investigation, response to data as "significant," and general framework of interpretation. As Siegman (1960) has pointed out, distinctions between "religious belief" and "religious behavior" must be made. Likewise, Allport (1960) has distinguished between "extrinsic" (second-hand, conformist, ethnocentric) religion and "intrinsic" (woven into one's life style, integral) religion and sought to develop a scale to assess these types on a single continuum. Lenski (1961) has distinguished between two "types of religious commitments . . . to a *socio-religious group* . . . [and] to a type of *religious orientation* which transcends socio-religious group lines." In the former, he has further distinguished between "communal" and "associational" involvement in religious groups and, in the latter, between "doctrinal orthodoxy" and "devotionalism." Though at some points his operational definitions appear inadequate, Lenski's study represents great advances in conceptual clarity.

There thus appears to be little real basis for religion remaining a taboo topic in social science. Methods and concepts are available for research of high empirical and theoretical quality. The research planning workshop held at Cornell University in the summer of 1961 under the auspices of the Religious Education Association showed that it is possible to bring together a multifaith, multidisciplinary group including religious educators and social scientists for an extended period for mutual benefit with the result of an impressive number of solid research designs as the basis of further personal and cooperative investigation (Cook, 1962a; 1962b).

Granting all of the above, it still remains true that religion (or, to be more precise, the faith commitment of the individual) is still a relatively taboo topic for the researcher and leaves him in a quandary about how to approach it. It is still difficult to disengage one's own commitments and anti-commitments when one enters the numinous realm, which by definition both fascinates and frightens. For researcher as well as for subject, these are significant issues, matters of importance and not simply of fact (Allport, 1955). Study of them usually operates to change them in one way or another; there are ethical dilemmas for the researcher involved as well as procedural problems. Yet, questions of meaning-value-commitment, of faith relationship to a Supreme Being in trusting dependence and ethical obedience (Jernigan, 1959), are or can be among the major determinants of an individual's life style, major ingredients in the "mix" of the psychic process. Social science cannot claim adequacy if it disregards religion.

▪ Selected Bibliography ▪

Allport, G.W. *The individual and his religion.* New York: Macmillan, 1950.

Allport, G.W. *Becoming: Basic considerations for a psychology of personality.* New Haven: Yale University Press, 1955.

Allport, G.W. *Personality and social encounter.* Boston: Beacon Press, 1960.

Bakan, D. *Sigmund Freud and the Jewish mystical tradition.* Princeton: Van Nostrand, 1958.

Clark, W.H. *The psychology of religion.* New York: Macmillan, 1958.

Collingwood, R.G. *The idea of history.* Oxford: The Clarendon Press, 1946.

Cook, S. W. (Ed.) Research plans formulated at the Research Planning Workshop on Religious and Character Education. New York: The Religious Education Association, 1962. (a)

Cook, S.W. (Ed.) Review of recent research bearing on religious and character formation. Research supplement to *Relig. Educ.*, 1962, 57, 1–174. (b)

Douglass, H.P., & Brunner, E. *The Protestant church as a social institution.* New York: Institute of Social and Religious Research, 1935.

Erikson, E.H. *Young man Luther.* New York: Norton, 1958.

Festinger, L., Riecken, H.W., & Schachter, S. *When prophecy fails.* Minneapolis: University of Minnesota Press, 1956.

Frazer, J.G. *The golden bough* [1890]. In T.H. Gaster (Ed.), *The new golden bough.* New York: Criterion Books, 1959.

Freud, S. *The future of an illusion.* New York: Liveright Publishing Co., 1928.

Hiltner, S. Pastoral theology in the schools. 1943. Mimeographed.

Honigsheim, P. Sociology of religion: Complementary analyses of religious institutions. In H. Becker & A. Boskoff (Eds.), *Modern sociological theory.* New York: Dryden Press, 1957.

James, W. *The varieties of religious experience.* New York: Longmans, Green & Co., 1903.

Jernigan, H.L. The meaning of faith: A theological and psychological study. Unpublished doctoral dissertation, Northwestern University, 1959.

Johnson, P.E. *Psychology of religion.* (Rev.) Nashville: Abingdon, 1959.

Jung, C.G. *Psychology and religion: West and east.* Vol. II. *Collected Works.* New York: Pantheon Books, 1958.

Kluckhohn, C.K. *Mirror for man.* New York: McGraw-Hill, 1949.

Lenski, G. *The religious factor.* Garden City, N.Y.: Doubleday & Co., 1961.

Malinowski, B. Magic, science, and religion. In J. Needham (Ed.), *Science, religion and reality.* New York: Macmillan, 1925.

Maslow, A.H. (Ed.) *New knowledge in human values.* New York: Harper & Brothers, 1959.

Moberg, D. O. *The church as a social institution.* Englewood Cliffs, N.J.: Prentice-Hall, 1962.

Muelder, W.G. Norms and valuations in social science. In A.N. Wilder (Ed.), *Liberal learning and religion.* New York: Harper & Brothers, 1951.

Murray, H.A. Studies of stressful interpersonal disputations. *Amer. Psychol.,* 1963, 18, 28–36.

Myrdal, G. *An American dilemma.* New York: Harper, 1943.

Parsons, T. *The social system.* Glencoe, Ill.: The Free Press, 1951.

Pratt, J.B. The psychology of religion. *Harvard Theological Review,* 1908, 1. (Included in Strunk, O. *Readings in the psychology of religion.* Nashville: Abingdon, 1959.)

Sargant, W. *Battle for the mind.* Garden City, N.Y.: Doubleday & Co., 1957.

Schneider, L., & Dornbusch, S.M. *Popular religion: American inspirational literature.* Chicago: University of Chicago Press, 1958.

Siegman, A.W. Personality and socio-cultural variables associated with religious beliefs and observance. Symposium paper read at XVIth Interntl. Cong. of Psychol., June, 1960, Bonn, Germany.

Tisdale, J. Psychological value theory and research: 1930–1960. Unpublished doctoral dissertation, Boston University, 1961.

Hypnosis

John G. Watkins

Man is attracted by the bizarre. He may seek to experience such phenomena, but the fact that he enjoys contact with the unique situation does not at all mean that he wishes to understand it. Some things are to be comprehended; some are only to be felt. Man has always resisted integrating his feeling life with his intellectual life. So it is with hypnosis.

Hypnotic phenomena are characterized by their transcendental nature. The execution of posthypnotic suggestions by an unwitting subject, the unusual memory feats of the hypnotized patient, the re-experiencing of childhood behavior under hypnotic regression, the denial of pain under hypnosis, and the demonstration of hypnotic hallucinations strike the uninitiated as magical, as supernatural. Yet, though they respond with curiosity and awe to lurid articles describing miraculous cures by hypnosis, they do not wish to hear about serious hypnosis investigations.

The taboo seems to be directed more against research on hypnosis than against hypnosis itself. Even the scientist will often enjoy attending a hypnotic stage demonstration and, although admitting that the phenomena are real, still resist the initiating of research in the field by his university. Hypnosis, like the kept woman, is to be enjoyed but not introduced in respectable company.

The out-and-out quack often gets a better press than does the serious scientific investigator of hypnosis. Thus, a news magazine sent reporters and photographers to cover the convention of a national hypnosis society. The reporters gathered much material, but the magazine, after discovering that there were no sensational papers presented and that it was not permitted to photograph subjects in hypnosis, decided against publishing any report of the meetings.

The writer had occasion a few years ago while sitting in a theater audience observing a stage "mind reader" to ask that he submit to certain controls. The performer's demonstration actually involved the sensing of minor muscle movements by selected suggestible subjects who were unconsciously leading him to the sites of hidden objects. However, the suggestion of controls to the experiment was indignantly rejected by other members of the audience, and the writer found himself in an unpopular position. When we dream, we want complete freedom for our fantasies to follow our impulses. It is as if we are willing to abandon objective reality and indulge in fantasy, provided we are not asked to attempt any reconciliation of the two. Let him who would destroy our illusions beware.

Even scientifically trained people are inclined, in the face of unaccustomed hypnotic phenomena, to throw up their hands in abandonment of reality positions. A highly skilled internist, on witnessing a case of hypnotically alleviated pain in a terminal carcinoma patient, remarked: "It's black magic." The researcher in this field is thus attacking deeply personal attitudes of people who are willing to accept hypnosis if it is presented as something miraculous, but not if it is considered something scientific.

Hypnosis is a vehicle onto which people project unconscious

needs—magical needs, power needs, erotic needs. Like the un-structured ink blot, it is seen as that which is most deeply per-sonal. Nowhere is this more evident than in the motivations which induce both scientists and practitioners to study hypnosis. The need to dominate others, the need to startle, the need to overpower, the fantasies of sexual seduction, the need to play God are often found in the motivations of hypnotists. Where is there a young man who has not fantasied having the power which would cause beautiful girls to fall over and do his bidding? These needs are, fortunately, seldom achieved by hypnotists ex-cept in their fantasies.

Conversely, subjects often seek to be hypnotized in order to gratify exhibitionistic impulses. They may wish to be overpow-ered, to be passive, to be seduced, or, through identification, to participate in the omnipotence of the hypnotist. For some, hyp-nosis is equated with death. To surrender one's ego is to die. Death fears activated in some people by hypnosis (and in others by anesthesia) arouse the same kind of resistances which have been described by Feifel in his chapter. Such anxieties make con-trolled research more difficult and in fact pose new questions which are themselves in need of study. Thus, hypnosis is often approached irrationally by both subjects and hypnotists.

Hypnosis has had a history of boom and bust. Each cycle has repeated the stages of the previous one. The work of Franz Anton Mesmer in the late eighteenth century touched off a furor in France. A century later, another great rise in interest occurred. And, within the past decade, the number of popular articles, television programs, and news reports indicate a new cyclical peak. (Marcuse, 1963).

The sequence of events is usually as follows: A period of relative disinterest is broken by the studies or reported clinical cases of one or more outstanding individuals. Often these men had developed their interest by observing workers regarded as charlatans. In fact, the scientist often sought out the charlatan in order to expose him. A latent interest is often characterized in its early stages by violent opposition. The reputable professional worker came, saw, and was conquered. After his conversion, he threw himself into study, experimentation, and writing. A period of high enthusiasm would follow. Disciples were attracted to the great man and absorbed his teachings. However, he soon found that others would not read his papers, and their publication was achieved only with great difficulty. The followers next became unscientific and tended to forget their basic identification as scientists or physicians. They began to treat all and sundry conditions with hypnosis indiscriminately. The inevitable failures occurred. Interest was lost, and hypnosis once again sank into limbo. Clinical use of hypnosis was seldom accompanied by controlled scientific studies. The clinical approach failed to establish a validated body of fact which could withstand the diminution of overenthusiasm, thus leading at the end of each cycle to its temporary oblivion.

The words that great men say live after them, even when they are wrong. And the study of hypnosis has suffered from statements of Sigmund Freud, his daughter Anna, and other psychoanalytic workers associated with them (Kline, 1958). These views have tended to turn scientists against the practice. Freudian psychology has been most influential on American psychiatry, and when Freud wrote that hypnosis "by-passed the ego," brought only temporary cures, and that he made his progress in psychoanalysis only after he had abandoned the hypnotic method, many of his followers considered this an injunction against its use. These views, now considered untenable by serious workers in the field, have, however, been instrumental in causing professionals to avoid the area. It is easy to ignore what we do not understand.

Freud himself discovered unconscious phenomena through his work with Breuer in hypnosis. And yet Freud was not a good hypnotist. He did not enjoy the close personal relationship which the hypnotic state initiates and admitted that he put people on the couch because he could not endure having them stare at him. It should be noted that resistance to hypnosis also draws its power from the same source as that directed against psychoanalysis—the disinclination of people to accept the reality of unconscious processes, to admit that they are not fully masters of their own mental houses.

Attacks on hypnosis have not always been at its genuinely weak or vulnerable spots. Rather, side issues have often been used to justify its dismissal. Thus, in the investigations of Mesmer's practice, the French royal commission—which included such men as Benjamin Franklin; Antoine de Jussieu, the botanist; Joseph Guillotin; and Antoine Lavoisier, the discoverer of oxygen—condemned it because they could find no evidence of "animal magnetism," the term Mesmer used to explain the phenomena. The commission was content to drop the matter at that, even though admitting that the phenomena existed and had not been explained. Mesmer abandoned his practice in disgrace and left France.

John Elliotson in England and James Braid in Scotland suffered condemnation by both the medical profession and the clergy. The pages of *Lancet,* the British medical journal, were denied them. Later, in this country the eminent psychologist Clark Hull was criticized by his colleagues for daring to publish a book on research in hypnosis (1933), the first serious scientific work of its kind.

Perhaps hypnosis suffers as much from its most enthusiastic supporters as from its enemies. The former, by their uncritical application, initiate the booms which soon turn into busts when it cannot produce the miraculous results expected. The serious proponent is torn between application of accelerator or brake in his attempts to stimulate solid interest and support. Physicians and scientists have often rushed from complete skepticism to total embracing, in which they temporarily abandon their disciplinary identification and become "hypnotists." Hypnosis fails to gratify the unrealistic expectations they bring to it, and they turn away in disillusionment.

This brings us to consideration of the characteristics of those who hypnotize and of those who seek to be hypnotized. Any relationship is compounded from human needs, often unconscious ones. The sadist and masochist find each other. The passive-dependent male seeks the phallic-aggressive woman in the taverns, and he who needs to be taken from is usually successful in contacting a thief. So it is with hypnosis. Men study hypnosis in order to explore the unknown (perhaps to gratify childhood frustrations of not being permitted in the parental bedroom), to manipulate, to seduce, all these, yet also the socially more desirable needs to understand and to help. Thus, the kind of subject or patient a given hypnotist attracts and holds in a hypnotic relationship must be one whose inner drives show some motivation complementary to his own. No wonder that hypnotic investigators disagree on who is hypnotizable or on what can be done in the hypnotic state. "Unconscious" speaks to "unconscious" through subliminal cues, and we often find in our subject what we seek.

We should hasten to note that such difficulties are inherent in all psychological experimentation. But it is only with hypnosis that the operator himself becomes such an integral part of the study that double human variables are introduced. The resistances and difficulties which confront the experimenter in this field come not only from the opposition, hostility, and fantasies of society and subject. They sprout equally from the unconscious trends of his own being. The writings of some investigators clearly display their insistent need to *prove* the reality of the hypnotic "magic." In others, the equally compulsive drives to debunk, to dispel the transcendental aspects of hypnosis, to show that there are none of its phenomena which cannot be duplicated without it are manifested. Many papers fervently adopt one side or another of the many controversies besetting the field. Less frequently, studies are reported which have caused their investigator to abandon previously held viewpoints. Perhaps the more "taboo" an area is, the greater the commitment to emotionally held attitudes toward it by its students.

Jealousies are rife among workers in hypnosis. It is not uncommon that a hypnotic demonstrator, teacher or therapist develops "possession-right" feelings about a good subject. He resents the subject's being given to another investigator or clinician. This jealousy over patients commonly occurs, of course, throughout the practice of medicine and dentistry. In hypnosis it is only intensified. Here, the transference nature of the hypnotic personal relationship is clearly demonstrated.

Hypnotists take great pride in their individual approaches. Societies, study groups, and disciples tend to develop around what has been called in the Soviet Union "the personality cult." An outstanding worker attracts others who, through identification, would participate in his "power." Such social formations are not abnormal. But they do make difficult the job of the objective, experimental scientist who would investigate hypnotic phenomena.

Not only is there this great variety of personality drives among hypnotists, but, complementarily, the subjects puckishly show variation and inconsistency. They refuse to be the same person in the hypnotic laboratory relationship as they are in the hypnotic clinical relationship. Thus, the application of appropriate controls becomes a Herculean task.

Research centers in hypnosis, such as those at Stanford University and the universities of Michigan, Michigan State, Illinois, Harvard, and Indiana, are valiantly attempting to reach past these complicating conditions to discover the "true" nature of hypnosis itself. Whether we can discover its true nature apart from the nature of the individual experiencing it, is still a controversial question. In this taboo area, universals tend to elude our scrutiny.

The role of unconscious suggestion by the investigator needs most careful control. Thus, in one common controversy, that of whether antisocial behavior can be induced under hypnosis, some experimenters have reported only negative findings (Erickson, 1939); others seem to secure evidences of such behavior, at least as close as is possible without both hypnotist and subject being charged with crimes (Watkins, 1947). Yet the definitive studies in this area are yet to be done. It has been suggested that the needs of the researcher play a significant role in determining what types of behavior he can elicit. If he fervently believes that antisocial behavior cannot be induced under hypnosis, he unconsciously transmits subliminal cues to his subjects to negate his consciously given suggestions aimed at inducing such behavior.

If, as some hold, the hypnotic subject "introjects" the ego of the hypnotist, then an antisocial impulse in the hypnotist may cause his subject to act this out because he resonates to such an impulse. The "crime" is executed, and the hypnotist is gratified. With another experimenter, the defense against such criminal tendencies may be that which is transmitted. The subject "pleases" this second investigator by acting on the transmitted defense, rather than on the impulse. He refuses to carry out the suggested antisocial behavior. Thus, two scientists arrive at differing conclusions as to what is possible through hypnotic suggestion, although each may have employed carefully controlled experimental procedures under strictly scientific conditions.

Not only the subject but the hypnotist and the experimenter need simultaneous study if the hypnotic behavior which is induced is to be understood. Such controls are not usual in scientific investigation, the objectivity of the researcher being taken for granted. In all taboo fields, which are so fraught with emotional reactions, and in hypnosis in particular, which is such an intensely sensitive personal relationship, this objectivity cannot be assumed. The views of the chief contributors are well known. It is common that one picks up a new article by one of them and, before reading it, predicts its findings. This is not to question the sincerity of the experimentalists, but only to note that sincerity does not guarantee objectivity. Bias is exerted subliminally, unconsciously.

The problems requiring investigation are numerous. What do we mean by "depth" of hypnosis? To what extent are various hypnotic phenomena real and to what extent only "role-playing"? Can hypnotic regression be validated sufficiently to be used as a research method in the study of other psychological problems (Reiff & Scheerer, 1959)? What are the essential conditions of hypnotizability, and who is hypnotizable? How do induction techniques compare in relative effectiveness (Weitzenhoffer, 1957)? Can we develop some objective way of determining the appropriate technique for a given subject or patient? There are still more questions than answers.

There is a vast body of literature bearing on such questions, but it consists largely of clinical observations, individually reported experiences, and records of unusual manifestations. The number of studies which have been designed with good research methodology are few indeed (Barber, 1962). And those which have combined sound experimental design with clinical sensitivity are extremely rare. What is needed is a wedding of science and art. The reports of the clinical observer are rich with insights and suggestions. Alas, they seldom have controls and are often not replicable. As such, they cannot play a decisive role. And statistically controlled experiments by those naïve in hypnotic experience are often reduced to the meaningless counting of superficial manifestations.

As the interest of research foundations, great university centers, medical schools, and experimental clinics in hypnotism is stimulated—and it is definitely growing—we may see studies which incorporate sensitivity and objectivity; which cut through the welter of jealousies, transferences, and countertransferences, of personal fantasies and unhealthy inner motivations which are so pervasive in this deeply personal field and which so frustratingly impede the advancement of scientific understanding. As summarized elsewhere (Watkins, 1954):

> A true science of hypnotizing must be based on a deep and intimate knowledge of the personality structure of the patient, his transference needs, ego defenses and the cathexes (press-valence) of these factors. It would further require that the hypnotist be quite aware of his own countertransference needs, role abilities and limitations.

Further experience with hypnosis has not caused me to abandon any aspect of that statement. Rather, we can but ponder the tremendous difficulties and limitations which challenge our scientific search for a better comprehension of the hypnotic state in man.

■ Selected Bibliography ■

Barber, T.X. Experimental controls and the phenomena of hypnosis: A critique of hypnotic research methodology. *J. nerv. ment. Dis.*, 1962, 134, 493–505.

Erickson, M.H. An experimental investigation of the possible anti-social use of hypnosis. *Psychiatry*, 1939, 2, 391.

Hilgard, E., Weitzenhoffer, A., Landes, J., & Moore, Rosemarie K. The distribution of susceptibility to hypnosis in a student population: A study using the Stanford hypnotic susceptibility scale. *Psychol. Monogr.*, 1961, 75, No. 8.

Hull, C.L. *Hypnosis and suggestibility*. New York: D. Appleton-Century, 1933.

Kline, M.V. *Freud and hypnosis*. New York: Julian Press and The Institute for Research in Hypnosis Publication Society, 1958.

Marcuse, F.L. *The structure of world hypnosis*. Springfield, Ill.: Charles C Thomas, 1963, in press.

Reiff, R., & Scheerer, M. *Memory and hypnotic age regression*. New York: International Universities Press, 1959.

Watkins, J.G. Anti-social compulsions induced under hypnotic trance. *J. abnorm. soc. Psychol.*, 1947, 24, 108–119.

Watkins, J.G. Trance and transference. *J. clin. exp. Hypnosis*, 1954, 2, 284–290.

Weitzenhoffer, A.M. *General techniques of hypnotism*. New York: Grune & Stratton, 1957.

• 10 •

The Psychologist in International Affairs

Charles E. Osgood

This essay is divided into two parts. The first might be subtitled "How I Became a Hard-nosed Peacenik"; it is a personal report which I hope will be informative and perhaps encouraging to my colleagues. The second part will deal more directly with the if's, how's, when's, and where's of what has come to be called "peace research."

The reader will not find the word "taboo" mentioned in the body of the chapter. This is not to say that there is nothing taboo about peace, for, certainly, peace has become a highly emotionally charged topic, and taboos are characterized by blind and violent emotions. Peace, hopefully, however, has not yet become completely taboo, although there are enough similarities to cause unease. The university professor who becomes involved with political questions, as peace has now become, must know that he subjects himself to question and even suspicion. Background, affiliations, ideology—all come under scrutiny. Character, beliefs, convictions become fair game to critical people in government.

But if we are ever to enjoy peace and pursue the investigations into more specifically taboo topics, such as sex and death, we must be alive to do it. The headlong rush of peace toward the undesirable status of a taboo needs to be arrested. Instead, peace needs to be advanced, investigated, and understood, tasks to which I now find myself deeply committed.

PERSONAL

What ingredients are required to make an ordinary, self-satisfied experimental psychologist—with more scientific jobs planned than his life can encompass anyway—into a peacenik who spends nearly half his time writing, lecturing, consulting, and doing research aimed at reducing international tensions? One ingredient is felt concern about the significance of the problem; a second is felt efficacy; a third is having something to work for, a new alternative, an idea; and the fourth ingredient, I think, is some ability to run uphill.

Felt Concern

If one has a modicum of intelligence coupled with a modicum of imagination, it is not difficult to get concerned about the present world situation. No one who looks at the evidence and thinks about it can deny that: (1) never before in history have so few been able to destroy so many and so much in so short a time (indeed, there is no physical reason for not building a weapon that would irradiate the entire surface of the earth, and some say that we must do this because the Russians might); (2) nuclear weapons are almost entirely offensive, not defensive, in nature, and therefore the continuing arms race produces less, not greater, security; and (3) the only "defense" against the use of such weapons lies in mutual fear of annihilation—a fragile defense, indeed, humans being human.

Yet, how many intellectuals have lifted their brilliantly

plumed heads out of the sand and looked into the face of a nuclear holocaust? How many have asked themselves the traumatizing question: Of what value is present work if this larger problem is not solved? Why write this scholarly treatise on the hair styles of the ancient Egyptians if no one will be around to read it? Why run more rats through the maze if there will be no more human behavior or rat behavior to have a theory of? Some psychologists, being only human and subject to the laws of cognitive dissonance, will close this book firmly at this point. Yet, they cannot deny that almost instant elimination of everything they consider valuable is now possible in a way it never before in human history has been.

I claim my modicum of intelligence and my due share of imagination. Perhaps the fact that my father was a reader of science fiction had something to do with it. I began reading the old, large-size *Amazing Stories* in the attic at the age of eight. The end of the world and the details of its death throes—by a freezing flight away from the sun, by the evolution of strangling plants, as well as by self-annihilation with incredible weapons— became something conceivable for me. (I might add that about five years ago I stopped reading science fiction.) I believe that the capacity to hold in mind the probable nature and possible occurrence of nuclear war is one element necessary for active involvement in trying to do something about it.

But, in my case, at least, felt concern had another source as well. This was an intense devotion to rationality; I cannot think of any better way to say it. Annoyance with human irrationality has been a constant in my make-up (except, of course, when it is I who am irrational). For the first thirty years or so of my life, this was not directed in any way toward the political behavior of the human animal. I could not have cared less about national and international affairs. I did not even bother to vote.

In 1945, while I was working on the training of B-29 gunners at the Smoky Hill Army Air Force Base in Kansas, came announcement of our first use of an atomic bomb against Hiroshima, then soon after announcement of our second use against Nagasaki. I considered these acts both immoral and stupid, and

I still do. I suppose that I should have asked myself what I was doing training B-29 gunners, but I did not. Being still an avid science-fiction reader, I made dire predictions about the end of the world in a few years. My time scale was a bit off, as my wife has often reminded me, but such an eventuality is not becoming less probable. I even joined the Americans for Democratic Action to work on a special committee of the New Haven chapter for internationalizing control of nuclear energy and weapons. But when it became obvious that nothing along these lines was going to be accomplished quickly, I went back to being a struggling young psychologist.

And then McCarthyism struck home to me. When McCarthy began attacking academic freedom (which I had been taking more-or-less for granted), when he began destroying people with irrational smear techniques and was obviously getting away with it, I came charging out of my scholarly cave like a wounded bear. I began *reading* the newspaper, including columns and editorials, rather than just glancing at the headlines and enjoying my favorite comics. This just jangled my rationality factor all the more. Occasionally I would get angry enough to write a letter to the editor. I even made an outline and began collecting clippings, for a book aimed at McCarthyism and all it represented. I am certain that McCarthy had similar effects on many of us. But McCarthy finally picked the wrong target, got his "comeuppance," and went the way of all flesh. And I went back to psycholinguistics, still muttering and growling at what I saw in the newspapers and on television.

Felt Efficacy

Concern at the irrationality of man and the extraordinary danger of such irrationality in a world of competing nation-states armed with nuclear weapons are not enough. One must also feel capable of doing something about them. This comes partly, I think, from self-confidence and security in one's own profession; it comes partly from the discovery that some people, at least, are willing to listen. Of course, some would say that it takes a fool who is willing to rush in where wise men fear to tread.

In 1958, I had a chance to spend a year at the Center for Advanced Study in the Behavioral Sciences. It was an opportunity to get disentangled from the usual routines of academic life and to get entangled with the ideas of fifty other Fellows. I went there to write a book on psycholinguistics; I never wrote a word of it. I hardly opened the twenty or so fat folders containing materials for its various chapters. I did a variety of minor scholarly jobs, but the main reason the book did not get written (it still is not) was that I found myself in an office next to Jerome Frank, a psychiatrist from Johns Hopkins. Jerry shared my concern, but he was doing something about it. He had already written an article for the *Atlantic* that had had great impact, and he was preparing to serve as a witness before the Humphrey Subcommittee on Disarmament.

This was the catalyst I needed, but had not been looking for. It threw me into the most severe conflict I have ever suffered. For years, I had been saying "What can I do?" as a means of convincing myself that I could not do anything, which is a wonderful rationalization for going on with the research that might make no difference and the book that no one might read. Yet here was a constant reminder that one could do something relevant and even get people to listen. The more I looked at my own areas of competence in psychology—human learning, the dynamics of human thinking, and human communication—the more relevance I began to see. More than this, I convinced myself that the psychological factors in international relations, though by no means the whole story, were particularly significant precisely because they were so largely unrecognized.

A New Alternative

The kind of action into which one is thrust by the combination of concern and felt efficacy depends on who one is. It thrusts some into joining protest marches, signing petitions, and even howling at the moon in sheer outrage. It thrusts others into direct political action. It is most likely to thrust the scientist or scholar into *his* characteristic problem-solving activities—reading, talking, researching, and writing. So we set up a weekly seminar at the center on "Social Science Aspects of Policy in a Nuclear Age;" it included lawyers, economists, sociologists, anthropologists, a few political scientists, and almost every foreign scholar resident that year. We read the literature, talked informally, wrote papers and read them to each other, and, since a broad spectrum of opinion was represented, occasionally became embroiled in heated debate.

I began as an ardent unilateral disarmer. It seemed perfectly logical to me that, if one side threw away its weapons, the other would soon follow suit. Just as we would not leap to destroy a disarmed Russia with nuclear weapons, neither would it leap to destroy us. I felt confident that we could win the real war for men's minds by nonmilitary means in a disarmed world. In fact, I believed that a nonthreatening, economically healthy, and openly communicating environment would gradually serve to strengthen democratic as against totalitarian ways of life, both at home and abroad. I still believe these things.

But now we come to the hardening of this peacenik. When I sat down to write out my ideas for presentation to the seminar —my first paper in this area, entitled "Suggestions for Winning the Real War with Communism"—and kept trying them out on my colleagues over coffee in the California sunshine, it became perfectly clear that, logical or not, ordinary unilateral disarmament simply was not feasible. My own arguments about the irrationality of human thinking under stress—such mechanisms as denial, semantic remoteness of concepts, projection, psychologic, and stereotypy in perceiving alternatives—which I used to characterize the Cold War mentality also offered apparently insurmountable obstacles to acceptance of any nonviolent resolution of international conflict. I became obsessed with the criterion of *feasibility*. The problem became to devise and justify a strategy that could move us toward a more peaceful world and reduce the likelihood of nuclear weapons being used, yet operate within reasonable limits of national security as perceived by people in decision-making positions.

The original paper introduced the basic ideas of "Graduated and Reciprocated Initiatives in Tension-Reduction" (which, in the way of such things, is now usually referred to as GRIT). It met solid criticism from participants in the seminar and from others to whom I sent it, but it also generated interest as a somewhat novel policy idea. So I went back to the typewriter to try to meet the criticisms. The next major version was published in *The Liberal Papers,* edited by James Roosevelt, and was entitled "Reciprocal Initiative." The book was seized upon by the Republican National Committee as campaign material; it called the book "the Democratic plan for surrender" and my particular contribution, "surrender on the installment plan." But, with an assist from "The Ev and Charlie Show," they also helped make the book a best-selling paperback.

This book, coupled with my own distribution efforts, began to bring these ideas to the attention of hard-nosed but equally dedicated and concerned people both in and out of government. (It also brought my correspondence to a level where it could not be handled.) I discovered that once one gets his nose up into that atmosphere, it serves as a lightning rod, attracting all kinds of things—good and useful things, such as lecturing opportunities and consulting activities, but also bad and wasteful things, such as letters from crackpots and invitations to too many conferences. These experiences and contacts gave me an even clearer idea of the weaknesses and strengths of my own proposal, however.

The most recent version of the plan is a fairly hard-nosed job, I think. It is a paperback published by the University of Illinois Press entitled *An Alternative to War or Surrender.* The subtitle in my own mind was "Osgood's Last Gasp," but it probably will not be. It accepts the necessity of temporarily retaining our capacity for nuclear retaliation, but proposes using this capacity as a security base from which to take limited risks in the direction of tension-reduction, rather than using it merely as a deterrent. It accepts the necessity of temporarily retaining diversified conventional forces to firmly resist aggressive probes by an opponent (the "stick") while applying a pattern of deliberate initiatives designed to reduce and control tensions (the "carrot"). It elaborates in considerable detail the strategy and tactics of GRIT—how to create and maintain the right kind of credibility (firm but potentially cooperative), how to induce reciprocation by an opponent, how to design and execute programs of independent initiatives.

But there is still at least one aspect needing tightening. I am becoming convinced that the most complex and difficult problems we face in trying to ease out of the present, dangerous situation are internal rather than external. How can the irrational cries of "appeasement" and "surrender" be handled? How can the quite rational but short-sighted use of foreign affairs as political football be managed? How can the self-fulfilling but vicious cycles of the military, industrial, and scientific complexes, energized by billions of dollars a year, be slowed and reversed? To borrow an insightful tennis analogy from the Princeton sovietologist, Robert Tucker: we are engaged in doubles, not singles; on each side there is an irrational player who wants to beat the other side at any cost, including breaking up the game, and on each side there is a rational player who wants to keep the game going and win within the rules; paradoxically, the rational players have to play in such a way as to keep their opposite numbers in control of the game, which means sometimes giving them spectacular points.

Ability to Run Uphill

I know that this sounds like patting oneself on the back, but I cannot claim to have got very far up. An ant at the bottom of a teacup has no place to go but up. The fact of the matter is that, when one has an unconventional idea in a political area of intense feeling and must get the idea moving through the complex and curious mass media, he has an uphill battle on his hands. He tries to reach the minds of key people in the decision-making process (decidedly uphill!) while at the same time, by writing and lecturing, tries to reach the general public. With one hand he does research or supports research that seems to have a critical bearing on the major issues, while with the other he acts like a lobbyist and applies what he thinks he already knows. He is simultaneously impelled by the urgency of the issue and restrained by the necessity (if he is to be effective) of maintaining his balance and dignity as a scientist and scholar.

I am often asked such questions as: "Are you getting anywhere?" "Are your ideas having influence in Washington?" "Is anyone listening?" These are difficult questions to answer, for several reasons. For one thing, it is easy to overestimate one's own influence, to indulge in wishful thinking. When a pattern of events, such as the handling of the Cuban crisis and its aftermath, looks like what one has been suggesting, it is only too easy to assume that one's advice has been taken, when, in fact, the advisers are many and the possible reasons for actions multiple. For another thing, I suspect that, even if unconventional policy ideas are eventually to be successful, they will become so in a fashion analogous to "sleeper effects" in attitude-change studies; that is, they will have their first effects quietly in the minds of men, and, only when enough people are thinking differently and the time is ripe, will the unconventional approach achieve public acceptance. All of which, of course, assumes that the unconventional ideas in question have merit and *should* be accepted by the public and by leadership.

Is anyone listening? This much I can say: a great number of people, both in and out of government, have been exposed to GRIT by one means or another; how seriously it is taken and how much weight it has in competition with more conventional policy ideas, I cannot say. The entire notion of independent United States initiatives in arms control and tension control now appears to be respectable, although I cannot by any means claim sole responsibility for this. Several sizable research projects, some supported by government agencies and others by private funds, are now investigating the feasibility of unilateral initiatives. What does all this add up to? Not much, but it is something. I realize that this first section reads like the story of a one-man battle. It is not; there are constantly increasing numbers of people going the same general direction and working just as hard or harder.

PROFESSIONAL

It may be professional myopia, but I think that psychologists as a group have been more actively involved in "peace research" and over a longer period than any other behavioral or social science. For a long time, we have had the Society for the Psychological Study of Social Issues, whose members have done research and written about problems in such areas of public concern as race relations, civil rights, and peace and war. More recently, in 1960, beginning with a "working group" under Roger Russell, a continuing committee for the profession as a whole on Psychology in National and International Affairs was established. Members of this committee have been Raymond Bauer, Urie Bronfenbrenner, Morton Deutsch, Fred Fiedler, Harold Guetzkow, John Finan, Ed Hollander, Herbert Kelman, Joseph Weitz, and I, but this represents only a small sample of the professional psychologists actually involved. Most recently, through a grant from the Marshall Fund, we have been able to support a full-time person, Larry Solomon, in Washington to work on the committee's tasks.

Why should it be so, if indeed it is, that psychologists have got themselves involved in this earlier and more deeply? Perhaps it is because psychology had about the right "distance" from public issues—close enough to have developed a scientific conception of man and his behavior, but not so close as to have become intimidated. Perhaps the fact that psychology is more like the physical and biological sciences in method and in quantification created a feeling of security and efficacy. In the past few decades, psychologists have been quite self-conscious about scientific methods and have generally convinced themselves that, "even though they may not know the answers, they know how to find out." Or perhaps it is the outward-reaching tendencies of psychological theories of behavior, which may have their moorings in the Skinner box, the tachistoscope, or the therapeutic interview, but are generalized as much as possible.

The natural, legitimate tendency of a theory to generalize carries with it the real danger of overgeneralization. Put less kindly, psychologists face the danger of "overselling" wares which they may not have. This has been a constant concern of the Committee on National and International Affairs. There is nothing that would more effectively undercut the potential contribution of psychology to public affairs than repeated failure to follow through on explicit commitments to solve practical governmental problems. This is probably why professional psychologists have preferred to advertise themselves as equipped to do research, rather than to promise solutions or even advise from a body of established principle. And the danger here, of course, is that of leaning over so far backward to avoid "overselling" that we rule ourselves out for real contributions we might well be able to make. The committee has tried to steer between these two reefs.

The psychologist working on public issues may wear any of three hats, but he should be aware of which hat is appropriate for which occasion. On some occasions, he may legitimately don his "professional" hat—when he speaks as a psychological scientist on the basis of hard facts and generally accepted principles. On other occasions, he should wear his "specialist" hat—when he speaks as an individual psychologist who, by virtue of his special training and experience, may claim a higher probability of correct insights and opinions in certain areas than those not so trained. On yet other occasions, he must explicitly display his "citizen" hat—when he speaks his opinions, expresses his attitudes, and takes his stand on matters where neither his science nor his expertise give him any obvious advantage over other equally intelligent citizens.

An example of this arose in the meetings of the APA Council several years ago. There was strong pressure from some members for the association to take a public stand against the United States resuming nuclear testing, following the resumption of testing by the Soviet Union. The committee's policy recommendation, which was finally accepted, was as follows:

The Association should speak for the psychological profession on social and political issues only when psychologists have a professional expertise which is clearly relevant to the issues involved and when there is a substantial convergence of judgment among psychologists on the nature and implications of relevant scientific data. There are, of course, many urgent issues in which the need for psychological knowledge is apparent. When such knowledge is not available, the Association should encourage research to foster its development. At all times, the Association maintains its traditional interest in having its members participate as individual psychologists and citizens in the presentation and discussion of psychological facts and ideas as they bear on current national and international problems.

The three hats I mentioned above are clearly described in this statement. It is not always easy to maintain these distinctions, and some will argue that, with an issue as urgent as avoiding nuclear war, trying to maintain them involves a delicacy verging on the ludicrous. The answer, I think, is that to fail to make these distinctions is to destroy whatever contribution we can make as psychologists.

There are two other caveats I must make before saying something about action and research on international affairs. One concerns what we mean by "peace." Perhaps it is because of the grinding process which I have been through in the search for feasibility, but I often get the feeeling that many of my colleagues have never thought very hard about what they mean by this term. It is the opposite of "war," which we are all against, and there surely is a good feel to it. But do we mean "peace" in the no-war sense? In the no-nuclear-war sense? In the complete-disarmament sense? In the permanent-tranquility sense? In the sense of establishing and observing the rule of international law? In the sense of peaceful (competitive) coexistence? In the *Pax Americana* sense? How one answers this question will determine what he includes under "peace research," how much effort he will put into short-term versus long-term action and research programs, and so forth. The controversy now going on between the "arms-management-and-control" proponents and the "general-and-complete-disarmament" proponents in part reflects differences in what kind of peaceful world people have in mind.

The other caveat concerns our own stereotypes and intolerance. Being merely human, psychologists are prone to the same cognitive dynamics they study in others. In our own striving for a simplified, comprehensible world, it is easy for us to set up bogeymen of our own—the Pentagon, Congress, the Mass Media, the Defense Industries, and so forth. Here are the Warmongers, here are the evil men who, for selfish and aggressive motives, are deliberately risking all our lives. There probably are a few such people, but I have yet to meet them. I have yet to find a person, in government, in industry, in the mass media, in the military, or elsewhere who does not profess to desire "peace" (on his own terms) as ardently as I do (on mine). We might differ absolutely on our assumptions and prescriptions, but not on our basic motives—to preserve both our lives and our way of life. But, most importantly (as we should realize as psychologists), to impugn these men's motives, to accuse them of being immoral and callous to the best interest of humanity as a whole, is promptly to establish an antagonism through which it is impossible to exert any positive influence. I do not want what I have just said to be misinterpreted. I am convinced that there are many people in the institutions we are discussing who are misguided, who have dangerous misconceptions about the nature of the world today and the nature of the people who inhabit it, and who are following policies that have a high probability of eventuating in the destruction of everything we hold valuable; but as a social scientist I cannot consider them evil, and I must consider them modifiable.

Action

By "action" for a more peaceful world, I refer to the whole spectrum of endeavors to change people's minds and thereby their behavior through utilizing what we know (or think we know) as psychologists and as intelligent citizens. It involves all the skills we have as individuals in personal relations, in persuasive communication, and in problem-solving. It means trying to inject psychological insights and skills wherever they are relevant; and often the first and most difficult step is to convince others of their relevance.

One type of action is, frankly, *lobbying,* in the best sense. By "best sense," I mean trying to influence decision-making in government for altruistic rather than selfish ends. I believe that there is a difference between lobbying for support of inter-American exchange among students and scholars and lobbying for higher status and pay for psychologists in government. Lobbying for increased support of research in the behavioral and social sciences would, I suppose, be equivocal. The Committee on National and International Affairs, particularly through the good offices of its full-time executive officer, Larry Solomon, has been trying to develop effective contacts with relevant government agencies and activities (Agency for International Development, Arms Control and Disarmament Agency, Peace Corps), as well as with members of Congress. One side of this activity is necessarily educational; it is surprising how many nonpsychologists, both in government and in the public at large, see us *only* as clinicians interested in and competent with personality problems. Another side of this activity is predictive—trying to anticipate public issues and prepare for them. Yet another side is a mediating role—bringing the public official with a problem and the psychologist with relevant skill and experience into fruitful contact.

Another type of action is trying to inject the psychologists' conception of the nature of man into the decision-making process. Again, being merely human, we tend to project our own conception onto others and are often shocked to discover how different other people's conceptions may be. Among the generally, if not completely, agreed-upon elements in the psychological conception of man are: man's behavior is determined by both innate and acquired factors and, as a kind of corollary, no individual is inherently evil; differences among individuals within nations, races, and the like are typically greater than differences between them; war is not inevitable, although many of its contributing elements (for example, aggression, fear, perceptual distortion under stress) may be; much of man's behavior, particularly as it relates to group solidarity and conflict, is learned and hence modifiable; and much of man's behavior is determined by irrational rather than rational factors. One means to inject our conception of man into the decision-making process is to bring psychologists into continuous contact with people in government; the APA committee has already made arrangements for several Congressional fellowships for psychologists, and we hope to have our own program under way soon.

Yet another type of action is the role of devil's advocate, questioning general assumptions. Examples of such assumptions are: that our opponent (whoever he may be) is motivated by aggression and hatred, whereas we are motivated by insecurity and fear; that we must maintain military superiority in order to be secure; that our nuclear deterrent is nothing more than that (it is also a security base from which to take limited risks); that credibility of our deterrent requires that we present the face of implacable hostility to an opponent; that prior commitment from both sides by means of negotiation is a prerequisite for tension-reducing action by either; and that we can have unlimited national sovereignty and unlimited international security at the same time. It is precisely because such assumptions are often implicit that they must be questioned and raised to the level of public debate. They create a rigid and narrow framework for policy, within which only a small number of possibilities seem to be available.

A sample of the activities undertaken by the Committee on National and International Affairs will serve to illustrate the variety of actions open to us. With support from the Brookings Institution, it was possible to hold four informal, two-day conferences among representatives of the mass media, government, and the universities on the general topic of communications and public policy, with different people participating in each conference. In connection with the Peace Research Institute, a working conference on the behavioral and social-science aspects of the Civilian Defense program was held, and a pamphlet called *The Shelter Centered Society* resulted. More widespread involvement of the profession as a whole is being pursued by developing a roster of psychologists competent and informed on various relevant topics, by arranging all-APA and divisional symposiums at regional and national meetings, and the like. Interprofessional cooperation in this area is being stimulated. Fruitful contacts with the United Nations Secretariat have been made, and a number of studies relevant to UN problems (particularly in the communications area) have been begun. An easy-access-and-retrieval coding and filing system for literature, personnel, and research proposals relevant to psychological factors in peace and war is being prepared. (For information on a monograph on this topic, see below.) It is hoped that such a facility will enable us to respond promptly to requests for digests and even position papers that come to us from people in government.

Research

Psychologists are as prone to fads as anyone else. There are fads in research. There was a period when learning theory was astride the white stallion; now it seems to be mathematical models. Young people quickly develop a sixth sense for what is "paying off" in job offers and promotions; a few regional and national meetings are sufficient to set a pattern, and such patterns are difficult to change over short periods. Although a great deal of research that has been going on steadily in social psychology, communications, cognitive processes, and many other areas is clearly relevant, "peace research," under that name, at least, is certainly not prestigious in our profession. However, the attractive power of a research area depends both on the stature of the senior people in it and on the availability of funds (which, incidentally, are not independent factors), and the situation seems to be becoming more favorable. Recent trips to university and other research centers throughout the country by my colleague, Shel Feldman, indicated a rather surprising density of relevant research, much of it quite explicitly (in the thinking of the investigators) on problems of war and peace, arms control, disarmament, international tensions, and related areas.[1]

[1] Papers describing these research projects can be obtained by writing to Dr. Shel Feldman, Institute of Communications Research, University of Illinois.

CHARLES E. OSGOOD

Action-oriented Research

Some research is designed to produce dependable information that can be translated directly into action programs. This is particularly characteristic of research oriented to public issues. One illustration is the monograph, *Psychological Factors in Peace and War,* being prepared by Shel Feldman, Joseph de Rivera, and me with the support of the National Institute of Mental Health and Earl Osborn, president of the Institute of International Order. The general purposes are to make available to behavioral and social scientists in a readily digestible form the existing evidence on psychological propositions explicitly or implicitly made in the literature in this field, the hypotheses that need investigation, and the available personnel in terms of contributions and interests.

Another example is the production of what might be called "instant public opinion" on foreign-policy issues and assumptions. Under Dee Norton's general direction, the Iowa City Consensus on International Affairs has been polling its membership on a variety of issues of the moment (for example, Proposition #4: "We urge the United States Government to take immediate steps to re-establish diplomatic, cultural and trade relations with Cuba") and transmitting the results to various people in government. The point is that decisions are often made on the basis of assumptions about "public opinion" that may well be invalid. If such informed opinion could be collected in synchronized fashion from a broad sample of the population, it could have impressive impact.[2]

[2] I once had the fantasy that there was a huge map of the United States on a building near the White House. Above the map, a flashing sign announced "The Issue of the Day." With each county in each state represented by a small panel that would be turned to either black or white depending on the responses obtained there, the whole map would represent, by shades from white through gray to black, "instant public opinion" on the issue, as well as regional variations. Congressmen and men in various agencies could not help but steal a peek at what was happening as they went to and from their offices; the mass media would obviously have to carry these displays as regularly as they now carry the weather maps; and, when visiting the capital, every Mr. and Mrs. Jones from Podunk would want to see the display and point to *their* community. Sheer fantasy, but it could easily be done.

Yet another illustration is a panel study done by Feldman and Fishbein at our institute of the performance of a peace candidate in the last election; he lost, to be sure, but the action-oriented research was designed to find out why.

Understanding-oriented Research

What we usually refer to as "pure," or "basic," research is directed toward increasing our understanding of human behavior without any immediate concern for social action. What impresses one when he starts searching the literature for material relevant to the present topic is the fact that, if one forgets the particular substantive material, almost everything we are investigating has some relevance. A William McGuire does ingenious experiments on susceptibility to, and immunization against, persuasion; the persuasive materials may be counter-arguments to unquestioned assumptions about the value of brushing one's teeth, but they might just as well have been counter-arguments to the unquestioned assumptions about national security listed above. The point is that there is much that we are doing already, just because we want to find out more about human beings—how they think, how they make decisions, and how they behave—that could be made directly relevant to the crucial issues of our time by a minor shift in materials, subjects, or emphasis.

Some will argue that it is impossible to be truly objective when the topics under investigation are policy-relevant, are emotion-laden, or involve the investigator himself. I think that this is sheer nonsense. As soon as one has become involved in his own theory, his mentor's theory, or even his own previous findings, he is equally liable to bias. The whole purpose of our training in rigorous, objective, quantitative methods is to protect ourselves from such bias, and objective methodology will protect us if adhered to.

Merely by way of illustration, here are some areas of understanding-oriented research which I think particularly relevant: the simulation of complex human decision-making processes, whether by computers (e.g., Herbert Simon's work) or by people (e.g., Harold Guetzkow's internation simulations); studies of the dynamics of human perception or cognition as they affect choice behaviors of all types (e.g., extending and refining the theories of Heider, Festinger, and others); research on interpersonal, intergroup, and internation communication (e.g., the problem of multiple audiences receiving the same message and that of information restriction because of the structure and function of the mass media); crosscultural and crosslinguistic studies of psycholinguistic and other cognitive phenomena, both as a means of quantifying what might be called "subjective culture" and as a means of specifying cultural similarities and differences more rigorously.

The principles and tools developed in the course of such understanding-oriented research could be transferred rather directly to the "applied" research that is needed by society. Take, for example, internation simulation (which is not very different from the "war games" played by the military). If the validity of such simulations can be demonstrated and they can be shown to significantly reduce uncertainty in policy decisions, one can imagine a massive program of such research designed to simulate and thereby anticipate critical decision points in the constantly expanding "near future." Our present transportation and communication technologies make crosscultural tests of hypotheses and international surveys entirely feasible; we no longer need be provincial in the behavioral and social sciences. Indeed, many of our hypotheses require testing against a crosscultural and crosslinguistic matrix in order to distinguish that which is culturally and linguistically unique from that which is common to the human species. Research on this scale would require a great deal of money, to be sure, but no more than is thrown away every time an experimental missile or space vehicle plops into the ocean as a failure.

■ Selected Bibliography ■

Osgood, C.E. Suggestions for winning the real war with communism. *J. Conflict Resol.*, 1959, 3, 295–325.

Osgood, C.E. *An alternative to war or surrender*. Urbana: University of Illinois Press, 1962.

Osgood, C.E. Questioning some unquestioned assumptions about national defense. *J. Arms Control*, 1963, 1, 2–13.

Roosevelt, J. (Ed.) *The liberal papers*. Garden City, N.Y.: Doubleday, 1961.

Russell, R., Bronfenbrenner, U., Deutsch, M., Frank, J., Katz, D., Milburn, T., Osgood, C.E., & Stagner, R. Psychology and policy in a nuclear age. *J. soc. Issues*, 1961, 17, 1–87.

Wright, Q., Evans, W., & Deutsch, M. (Eds.) *Preventing world war III: Some proposals*. New York: Simon and Schuster, 1962.

Index

A

Academy of Religion and Mental Health, 85

Accident:
certification of death, 38-39

Adler, A., 15, 20

Agency for International Development, 119

Aggression, frustrated, 4

Allport, G.W., 6, 9, 19-20, 67-69, 72, 74, 77-78, 87-88, 92-94

Alternative to War or Surrender, An, 112

American Journal of Sociology, 86

American Psychological Association, 6, 19, 85-86, 120-121
Committee on National and International Affairs, 115-116, 119-120
Council, 116-117
Education and Training Board, 19-20

American Sociological Association, 85

American Sociological Review, 86

American Soldier, The, 15

Americans for Democratic Action, 109

Anderson, H.H., 68, 77

Farberow   35195

Bradford Junior College Library
Bradford, Massachusetts

DATE DUE

OCT 31 '64		
NOV 25 '64		
NOV 24 '64		
DEC 13 '64		
FEB 13 '67		
MAR 18 '7̶~̶	DISCARDED	
MAR 27 '68		
NOV 19 '68		
MAR 17 '69		
FE 20 73	DISCARDED	
JE 20 74		
MY 18 '76		
DE 15 80		
DEC 1 9 1987		
MAR 27 '02		